Saint Lynn   JR,

Bless you as you ~~come~~

on the wall with our King!

THE
WARRIOR'S
WALK

Rejoicing in His River!

Ish Payne

Ish Payne

Endorsements

"As beautiful as ancient sailing ships in port are, with the craftsmanship of the wood, rigging, and mast, this is not their created purpose.

Our churches have become ports, full of fully rigged ships with no journey before them. Now is the hour to set sail—the sails are ready, the ship is manned—all that is lacking is the Warriors to set sail and hit the stormy seas. It is time for the church to take her place on the wall and stand in the Gap.

Pastor Ish brings home the call, Walk and Overcome..."

Pastor Rick Bonnette
Counseling Pastor, Church on the Rock, Wasilla, Alaska
www.churchontherock.org

My friend, Ish Payne asked me to review his book, The Warrior's Walk, and give some of my thoughts on the book.

Bottom line! I really liked it and urge all to read this work.

Ish uses his experience in boot camp as a Marine recruit to develop a theme that compares our growing relationship with Jesus Christ to that of a new warrior.

Because of my background I personally relate to this theme. A graduate of the United States Naval Academy, I completed nuclear power training and submarine training to enter the submarine service. I served on WWII diesel submarines as well as nuclear powered, Poseidon Missile submarines. Eventually I was Commanding Office of the USS Dolphin, a diesel powered, deep diving submarine. At one time the USS Dolphin boasted the claim of being the world's deepest diving submarine. After serving for twenty years I retired with the rank of Commander. The last seventeen years I have served as a Senior Pastor.

Time and space limit what I can say, nevertheless, there are several points that grabbed me in the reading that will hopefully encourage you to get the book and read it.

1. It is relevant for today. With all that is going on in the world, the economy, terrorism, good being called evil and evil being called good, it makes the firm point that we are in a war and need to operate as such.

2. The necessity to learn to hear and obey the voice of authority (Jesus Christ through the Holy Spirit). The following quote from the book is true. Not only in the military, but in our walk with the Lord.

"You have been safe here at Parris Island, but you won't be safe if you go 'in country, the country of living hell' (referring to Viet * Nam) where not only the bullets and RPG's will kill you, but the land-mines, poisoned rat holes and snake snares will kill, maim and cripple you. If you have not learned to hear the voice of authority here and to respond to that voice you will not only get hurt, but you will be a hazard to every other Marine in your unit".

3. A quote from Ish's wife Tonda: "God is not changing us to stay the same." You will understand that simple, yet profound statement as you read about the Warrior.

This book is a practical and useful tool to help you live and walk "The Warrior's Walk."

Wayne A. Clarke, CDR, USN (Ret)
Senior Pastor, His Dwelling Place Ministries
www.HisDwellingPlace.com

"The Warrior's Walk" is a must read for every believer that is ready to lay down their life for the cause of Christ (right in the middle of these troubling times). We all long to hear "Well done thy good and faithful servant." But after reading Ish Payne's latest and most timely book, if there ever is a faithful warrior that hears "Semper Fi" from the Lion of Judah, that warrior will be Ish Payne.

Ish is not only a dear friend that I've only known to function with the Father's heart and as a prophetic servant to the hurting and wounded, but as you will learn, through this book, God has taught Ish what discipline and sacrifice is all about. So as you "volunteer" to sign up for this anointed adventure of "The Warrior's Walk," can you ponder with some of your "band of brothers", this question? Will we be the church that truly counts the cost, and will you and I be ready to hear, obey, and walk in our destiny?

The Commander in Chief is waiting...

Randy Collins
Assistant Pastor / Orange County, Calif.
Founder of "Redeeming the Time"
Freedom and Restoration Ministry

Ish Payne is a servant to the body of Christ. I have known Ish & Tonda for many years. His insight and ministry has helped people in my church, and he has learned, through serving, how to bring renewal and transformation into many lives.

His first book "Life in the Red Zone" we still recommend to people fighting stress and difficulties in life. "The Warrior's Walk" is an exciting read from the 'spiritual' view point of a former Marine. May it encourage you to give your all to the one who gave His!

Steve Doerter
Senior Pastor
Grace Community Church
Cashiers, NC

The Warrior's Walk is an adventure that every believer who seeks to fulfill their Kingdom Destiny must read.

Ish is a master story teller who weaves together powerful stories that contain Kingdom wisdom with Christ centered principles for everyday life. This book will empower you to war unto VICTORY!

Pastor Phillip Fields
Founder and Director
www.GetRealMinistries.us

What I love most about this book is that it deals with the grit of life that touches so many people. I'm talking about things like child abuse, sexual abuse, abortion, etc.—issues that have become commonplace in our society and have affected so many people. Yet, few people in the church are addressing these issues because they don't understand the dynamics of them, they don't have the courage to deal with them, or the issues just seem too ugly to touch.

If your life has been negatively affected by these things and you are looking for help. I believe that this book will be a breath of hope for you.

In my opinion, the foundation of the whole message that Ish addresses in "The Warrior's Walk" is found in Chapter Nine, "Honor." I can't help but believe that if every disciple of Jesus would live out of the reality of honor, the House of God would be a House of Freedom!"

Michael Lubanovic
Outreach Pastor
Fire School/Fire Church
Concord, NC

I have known Ish for many years and consider it an honor to provide an endorsement for this book, "The Warrior's Walk." Ish is a man of deep honor and integrity as well as boundless energy and enthusiasm to serve God and see people set free! Ish and I share a common experience in having served our country. We swore to defend our country, to fight against its enemies and defeat them in order to preserve our liberty and freedom.

I was astonished at the implications as Ish describes very accurately the process involved in making a Marine. It begins with a decision and a commitment to establish a "change that is forever." There is a process established in Marine training and environment that runs a very close parallel to the principles and teachings of Jesus. The principles and truth that becomes first nature to Marines, creates an atmosphere of love that manifests itself in devotion to duty.

Ish's description of the drill instructor walking through the barracks at night, with tears in his eyes, is a testimony to the bond that exists between Marines. Marines have a dedication in battle displayed by laying down their lives in defense of their comrades. Marines have vowed to never leave a fellow Marine wounded on the battlefield, or as a casualty. They will go to any length to bring them home. The spiritual implications and parallels are very significant and Ish takes time to explore the depth and direction of our Christian commitment. Ish describes the profound parallels between his story of becoming a Marine and becoming a Warrior for God.

There are examples of dedication, a change of nature and what a warrior would be confronted with in order to defeat the enemy and set the captives free. Marines know who they are; and accept their calling and have an inspiring devotion for the group.

Though no longer on active duty in the Marine Corps, these qualities express the devotion of Ish's heart as well.

Manny Macias, USAF Col. Ret.

The Warrior's Walk
Copyright 2009
Restoring Hearts Ministries
PO Box 100
Indian Trail NC 28079

Printed in the United States of America
1st Edition 2009
2nd Edition Revised 2010

Type set, formatting and cover design:
Life Application Ministries Publication (LAMP)
P.O. Box 165
Mt. Aukum, CA 95656

Printer: createspace.com

To the Reader

Ish Payne
Restoring Hearts Ministries
PO Box 100
Indian Trail, NC 28079
www.Restoringhearts.net

Acknowledgments

My special thanks to the following people for their help in editing and proofing my manuscript.

- Tonda, my precious warrior wife!
- Taylor and Lexie, my sweet daughters!
- Ann Wild, my mother in law, one special lady!
- Jennifer Mao and Denise Faw, my dear friends!

May the Lord bless you for your faithfulness to "The Warrior's Walk". You are really special and I love you!

To Tom and Linda Lange who worked countless hours preparing this book for print. I love you folks!

To my ministry partners John and Pam Shergur and Deanne Day for your continued faithfulness in ministering the "Love War" through Restoring Hearts around the world.

To my cousin Hilda Sutherland—Thanks for breaking the bread of life with me in making this all possible. Hilda, we have been blessed with a spiritual heritage that taught us to love one another as He has loved us!

To my dear friends Gregg and Michele Forwerck, of Gregg Forwerck Photography for your creative work. Thanks Saints!

To the brothers and their wives who wrote an endorsement for this book.

- Rick and Trudy Bonnette
- Wayne & Chris Clarke
- Randy & Ellie Collins
- Steve & Joyce Doerter
- Phillip & Darlena Fields
- Michael & Lisa Lubanovic
- Manny & Donna Macias

These are valiant warriors who have been tested and found "faithful" in the heat of battle. These are part of the leadership of the remnant that will turn the world upside down.

Saint Ellie Collins—In my next book we have to tell your testimony. It's time lady warrior—many need to hear it!

To my Pastor and friend, McLean Faw—you have taught me what "honor" means and you have demonstrated the reality of "Complete not Compete." I am grateful for your love and the heart of the "Watchman" demonstrated in your life.

My eternal Thanks and love to God the Father, the Lord Jesus and the Holy Spirit. You know the tears that have flowed from me as I have seen "the mercy seat" where the blue flame of God's manifest Shekinah glory hovers. You are an awesome God and I love you.

Cover photograph "Carrying the wounded back to the beach" found on www.militaryspot.com/gallery, registered by: Jim's police, Dell City, Oklahoma.

The word "Viet * Nam" is used throughout the pages of this book displaying a "star" in the middle. This is a memorial to all the fallen and missing soldiers.

I dedicate this to all the men and women in our Armed Forces that have heard the call to be "Watchmen!" You have honored your God and you have honored your country!

"All have given some, and some have given all!"

The Warrior's Walk is also dedicated to all the Spiritual Warriors who faithfully declare His Word and "Stand on the Wall and in the Gap" for the Body of Christ and all the creation!

To those "unnamed" warriors that have stood with me in this journey to reveal His glory and co-labor with our King! You are mighty warriors and I am forever grateful for your love and for watching my back!

You know who you are!

"The Warrior's Walk"

This picture sums up what it means to live
"The Warrior's Walk!"

These children knew who to come to in the midst of the "fire-fight." These warriors had been trained to fight and protect the sheep. They are watchmen and sheepdogs! They are standing on the wall and in the gap for these children. They will give their life for these vulnerable ones if necessary and they will do it with great joy because they are men of honor..
Beloved, do you hear the call?
Do you see the commander in Chief standing at the front encouraging us into the battle?
Will it be easy?
Will it be comfortable?
Will it be safe?

No! A thousand times No! But it will be glorious and we will see the blue flame of His Shekinah Glory as you walk with Him standing on the Wall and in the Gap!

Come warriors lets join the fight!

Contents

"So I stationed armed guards at the most vulnerable places of the wall and assigned people by families with their swords, lances, and bows. After looking things over I stood up and spoke to the nobles, officials and everyone else:

Don't be afraid of them. Put your minds on the Master, great and awesome, and then fight for your brothers, your sons, your daughters, your wives and your homes."

Nehemiah 4:13-14 MSG

Preface

Come with me as we walk together through the harsh sands of Parris Island where we learn how to bury 'sand fleas;' and then on to the unimaginable horrors of an Egyptian dungeon where your existence was at the whim of a sadistic master.

Laugh with me as I recall the 'new way of smoking' learned by the arrogance and pride of unlearned youth.

Cry with me as I remember Gunnery Sgt. Jettie Rivers and Corpsmen Russell McGee who paid the ultimate sacrifice while serving "in country, the country of living hell." Their brother's lives were more important than their own!

The story of the Four Chaplains is a testimony of the grace of our God and what commitment, honor and sacrifice is all about.

Learn the "real cost" of following the King into battle as we see the over 12,000 martyrs that are killed each month. That is over 150,000 killed for Jesus sake in 2008!

Weep with me as we realize that much of what we call "church" is nothing more than "roasting Christian marshmallows" in the yard of a little white house with a picket fence around it.

Do you know what it means to spiritually "Neglect" that He might become "All in All?"

Rejoice, however, as we see that 70,000 people are coming to Christ each week in China in the midst of the persecution.

Weep with me as we look at "Iwo Jima" and realize that just as the flawed intelligence in that battle cost us many lives, that the flawed intelligence of spiritual warfare and apathy in the church today is costing tremendous damage, destruction and death.

Pray with me that we turn this around! We are on a slippery slope and He is calling us to repentance and sacrifice. Saints, "We Ain't Gonna like Losing!"

Learn with me as we look at ways to turn the tide of death to the reality of life through the life of our Savior, Redeemer, Healer and Restorer Jesus Christ.

Read about "combat training" and how it relates to your walk with God. Let's study together one of the Kingdom keys which is the "toilet bowl brush." I promise it will change your life.

Why is the statement "God is not changing us to stay the same" so timely? Are you a stagnant yucky pool of water or a flowing river of love? Knowing the difference can be the difference between freedom and bondage.

Run with me to the sound of battle to "Advance" our position and "Occupy" where the darkness has ruled through the desolation of many generations.

Find out if you are a sheep or a sheepdog and ask God to give you His courage to "Stand in the Gap" and "On the Wall."

Hear with me the roar of the "Lion of Judah" and Come, learn how to FIGHT!

Introduction

The air was charged with nervous excitement as the chartered bus moved through Tennessee, Georgia, and South Carolina stopping at different towns along the way to pick up the young men. Never had I seen such a rag tag group of guys. We had everything on our bus from inner city hoods from Atlanta and Philadelphia to the son of a Fortune 500 company founder. None of us really had anything in common except we had all volunteered (some under duress of jail time) and all of us were headed for the same destination. Our destination was going to change our destiny and none of us had a clue what was in store for us. We were all volunteers and rattling with nervous excited chatter about the decision to volunteer. For me the decision was made on the banks of the Tennessee River as I had contemplated my future only ten days before. Now here I was on a one way journey—no turning back!

The bus lumbered east through the dark of night as the scenery became more and more barren and desolate, only broken by an occasional distant porch light seemingly like a lone firefly in the blackness. Dawn was approaching and we were all weary, but too wired to sleep.

My brain seemed scattered as I pondered the last year of my life—my freshman year at the University of Tennessee—getting to know the dean of students too well, he had suggested I contemplate another direction in my life until I knew who I was and where I was headed! Actually, he made it a mandate that I leave campus. He let me withdraw from school on good terms, but withdraw I must, or the option was the boot! That was really good advice since I had been heading in a number of directions, and most of them dangerous. The last straw for the dean had been my involvement in a Honky-Tonk bar brawl in a rowdy dive known as the Black

Poodle—my ear had almost been torn off when I got hit from behind with a lead loaded blackjack.

My thoughts were tugged back to the present as we rolled through Port Royal along the flat causeway of Highway 280 leading to the island, and then suddenly right ahead of me was a sign that read:

Welcome

To

Parris Island

"We make Marines"

My life was about to change! The Marine Corps recruiter said that the plan is to "establish a change that is forever" and that proved to be true!

We then approached the main gate and were waved through by the sentry on duty. Our next stop, a place I later learned was known as receiving, and as soon as that drill instructor stepped on that bus it got a little crazy! He let us know, in no uncertain terms that we were his property and property of the Corps and that instant and unrelenting obedience was not only wanted, but required, to live another day without facing unmentionable peril and distress!

His first order for us was to exit the bus and line up on the yellow footprints. The yellow footprints were painted on the pavement in exactly the proper formation for a platoon. He and the other drill inspectors wasted no time in establishing their absolute authority and demonstrated that any infraction would produce immediate regret! Within moments we experienced our first "sand flea burial service," and it was hard to bury the flea on the pavement! We were told to stand at attention with absolutely no movement. I was fortunate as I had six years of military school experience so I had some basic disciplines and understanding. As I was standing ram rod straight with my eyes straight ahead a guy next to me casually swatted at a sand flea. Big mistake! He was immediately put into the "push up position" where he started his first set of 100 push-ups. The closer you are to the ground the more the sand fleas bite you, and their bite feels like a tattoo gun shooting small barbs of searing red ink into your body.

He had barely started doing the push ups when he stopped and swatted at a sand flea biting his face. Bigger mistake! He was now directed to find that flea and prepare it for burial—he couldn't find it so recruits next to him (including me) were directed to assist in the search operation! It was real chaos as we were trying to do something that is impossible, but as we slowed down we were now doing push ups and being "thumped" as a reminder of who was in charge! By then other fleas had been swatted and the "search and bury" mission enlarged with every second! We finally managed to retrieve some of the dead fleas and proceed to the burial ground. The burial ground was a clump of dirt about 10 feet from the pavement. The original flea swatter was told to dig a grave in preparation for the service. Of course he reminded the DI's (Drill Instructors) that he had no tool to dig with and that was probably his biggest mistake! Of course he had tools—he had his hands and fingers. Because he was running his mouth with the DI's they learned his name right away. He was then asked if he thought they were stupid for such a command and he still did not have enough savvy to answer an unanswerable question in the right manner. With each question and each answer he kept digging himself into a deeper hole and certainly got off to a bad start with the DI's. Before this exercise was over each man in our platoon of 80 recruits had participated in the burial service.

It was not until much later that I got the revelation of what the DI's were doing. They were taking a bunch of individuals (some misfits and clowns) who had their own ideas, culture, thoughts, and levels of education and family values. They were molding them, transforming them, developing them and training them so they would learn to flow in unity and immediately obey the voice of the DI without question!

It reminds me of the words of the apostle Paul when he said: *"And He himself gave some to be apostles, some prophets, some evangelists, and some pastors and teachers for the equipping of the saints for the work of the ministry, for the edifying of the body of Christ, till we all come to the unity of the faith and of the knowledge of the son of God, to a perfect man, to the measure of the fullness of Christ. That we should no longer be children, tossed to and fro and carried about with every wind of doctrine, by the trickery of men, in the cunning craftiness of deceitful plotting, but, speaking the truth in love, may grow up in all things into Him who is the head—even Christ—from whom the whole body joined and knit together by what every joint supplies, according to the effective working by which every part does its share, causes growth of the body for the edifying of itself in love"* (Ephesians 4:11-16).

You see, they were trying to teach us was that we might be individuals and have special abilities, but we were nothing without the rest of the platoon. It was going to be all about teamwork, for we were either all going to pass or we were all going to fail. And failure was not an option! They were demanding excellence—not perfection—but excellence. Just like the church and the body of Christ are supposed to function—we all have different gifts and callings, but if we do not learn to flow together in love—we will not make the high calling! If we do not learn to love and honor each other as individuals, and in that love and honor flow with corporate unity; we will never reveal the body of Christ to a desperate and dying world that is longing to see it and be set free!

Do you want to make the high calling?

As we look at the parallel experience of Marine warrior training we are also going to look at one of my favorite men in the Bible. His name is Joseph! We have no record that he was ever trained as a warrior, but a "Warrior's Walk" was what he demonstrated for us as he walked in victory under the worse possible conditions! Joseph was not a "chocolate soldier" but instead a man of great faith who walked in the favor of God and in the favor of man.

It has been said by Marine commanders that the "function of the Marine Corps is to locate, close with, and kill the enemy." Little did I know that years later I would look back on boot camp at Parris Island Marine Corps recruit training and understand the wonderful parallels to what our Father God is preparing us for; and that is for us to have...

"The Warrior's Walk"

"Count the Cost"

What does it mean to give?
When life is short, with only one to live,
To lay your life down at any cost,
For that's what Jesus did on the cross.

You see, He heard the Father say "count the cost"
Obedience required it or all would have been lost,
He walked that way for all the world to see,
The creation now looks for that walk in you and me.

Can we say we love Him and yet do less?
Than give our all to Him including our best,
Our life is a vapor, it goes fleeting by,
If we grasp and cling to it we shall surely die.

Can a grain of corn bring forth life lying on the earth?
Does it not have to be buried to bring forth new birth?
Faithful is the saint who does not faint nor falter
For resurrection life is gained by laying it on the altar
What does it mean to give?
When life is short, with only one to live
We begin the journey by counting the cost,
The prize is to walk with Jesus, our glory the cross!

Ish Payne

Chapter One

No draftees in this Fighting Force!

The dictionary defines decision as "a judgment or conclusion reached, the act of making up one's mind." Every young man on that bus had made a decision that he wanted to be a part of the Marine Corp. No one had forced them to join. No one had been drafted. They had all volunteered following a decision of their own will. Yes, a few of them were in trouble with the law, but they could have chosen a different route to satisfy the judge. Some joined because they thought the Marines had the best looking uniforms (they do) and some joined because they wanted to be a part of the very best—**"The Few and the Proud"**! That was my case. If I was going to commit to military service I wanted to learn how to be a warrior and I knew that the Marines would teach me the skills to survive.

I, Me or Mine!

The problem was that none of us realized in order to make warriors out of us it would be necessary to totally change our thinking. We were going to be required to have our minds renewed in order to think in a totally new way. A big key was that no longer were the words "I, Me or Mine" going to be a part of our vocabulary. Now it was no longer just about the individual, but it was about the unit or the team. We were going to learn to work together to accomplish the mission and "working together" was foreign to all our young minds. Young men that had never done anything for anyone would learn to help their fellow recruits clean their weapons, make the rack (bed) so you could bounce a quarter off it, study for tests, etc. All the while the recruits usually didn't even know they were learning to be a part of something much bigger than themselves, but were learning the joy of "giving."

Well, being a volunteer suddenly became a problem for some of these guys. They quickly started realizing **they were not their own**, but had **volunteered** to be a part of something much bigger that might actually cost them their life! Yes! Their very life! For many, it was the first real commitment they ever made and they knew that in order to make it they were going to have to get with the program. And many didn't like the program! You see, the program required 100% commitment, effort, and obedience, and when I say obedience, I mean **instant obedience**. Anything less than instant obedience would produce **instant regret** of some kind!

Cigarettes! A new way of smoking!

Immediately after the burial of the sand fleas we were herded into a large room known as receiving. This was where we would exchange all of our own clothes for standard military fatigues, and be issued basic products such as toothbrush, toothpaste, razor, shaving cream, etc. All of our own personal stuff was boxed and shipped to our home address. When they were through with this exchange we had nothing left that was personal (other than a Bible or wedding ring) and we were all dressed alike! The transformation had begun!

We were all standing at attention in this room together in platoon formation when the DI asked if there was anyone who wanted cigarettes. He said "This is your last chance; if you want cigarettes you have to get them now." I knew this was some kind of trick, because the former Marines that I had talked to before getting there had told me that there was not going to be any smoking, eating candy, or drinking soft drinks, as they were determined to get us into the best physical shape possible. Well, there was this young fellow in the back of the room who raised his hand and said "I want some cigarettes." The DI ordered him up front and asked him "do you prefer filter or non-filtered cigarettes?" The recruit answered very politely and said "non-filtered Sir." The DI then handed him a pack of non-filtered cigarettes and said "now open them and put one in your mouth." You could tell by the smug look on the recruit's face that he thought he had been the only one smart enough and brave enough to say, "Yes, I want cigarettes." The recruit was now standing in front of all of us with the cigarette dangling from his mouth when the DI said to him "are you sure you want that cigarette?" "Yes Sir" the recruit answered "I want it!" The DI then said "Well good, since you want it you can have it; now EAT it!"

There then began a barrage of comical facial expressions worthy of a Broadway show! A candid camera type show would have loved to have recorded the different expressions on the recruit's face. No more smugness, no more vain glory, no more conceit, no more pride, no more arrogance; only total wide eyed disbelief! "Eat it?" The recruit said. "Yes, eat it!" The DI said. The recruit replied, "But sir cigarettes are made for smoking!" "Not in my platoon" the DI said. "In my platoon cigarettes are made for eating, not smoking. Now eat it!" And eat it he did! And it ate him, for it was not long till he was running to the door sick!

A half dozen other recruits had made the mistake of laughing while this exercise was going on and they to were called up front and commanded to share in the eating of the recruit's cigarettes. You see they were supposed to be at attention, not laughing!

We were learning the important lesson that any disobedience produced **instant regret!**

The message was coming through **loud and clear** that we were only to listen to the voice of the DI. And total and

11

complete obedience to that voice was required! It sounds simple, but when you have lived all your life doing your own thing saying—I want, what I want, when I want it—then listening and obeying is a whole new experience!

The reality of volunteering or enlisting was becoming clearer and clearer with each moment. We were beginning to understand that there was a definite **cost** involved!

Volunteer versus drafted!

What had we volunteered for? What was it going to cost?

- To have a new commander in our life

- To come under the authority of new leadership

- To be changed and become a person of honor

- To learn to move as "one new man"

- To learn the joy of living in unpredictable circumstances while trusting your leader

- To reflect a glory that was not our own

- To become a "warrior" who could help liberate those that are oppressed, captured, and prisoners of war

- To experience the furnace of shared hardships and grow as a result of it

- To consider our fellow Marine more important than our self

- To represent a "high calling" much higher than our selves or our individuality

You must be a volunteer to be in the army of our Lord—

draftees won't cut it!

A volunteer has made a decision that they want to "join" and be a part of something larger than themselves and they do so willingly. A draftee is forced, but a volunteer joins.

Tragically, the church today has many draftees. They came because their parents made them, their spouse made them, or, as a friend of mine confided to me, "I joined the church so I could add church membership to my résumé."

It is no mystery why there is a lack of power in the western church when we see the draftees that are holding down pews week after week waiting for something to happen, while at the same time not believing that anything is going to happen. To them it is business as usual, but kingdom warriors will settle for nothing less than "Heaven Invading Earth!" [1]Before an army can occupy, it must first invade and be trained how to bind the "strongman" described in Matthew 12:29 which we will look at in Chapter Ten.

As the old chorus said, "It is a battlefield, brother, not a recreation hall" and our Father has ordained a **boot camp** for the volunteers that want to become vessels of honor.

Jesus made it clear in teaching on the cost to follow Him when He said *"What king, going to make war against another king, does not sit down first and consider whether he is able with ten thousand to meet him who comes against him with twenty thousand? Or else, while the other is still a great way off, he sends a delegation and asks conditions of peace. So likewise, whoever of you does not forsake all that he has cannot be My disciple"* (Luke 14:31-33).

Volunteer = Repentance

It was actually years later I realized that when I volunteered for the Marine Corps that I could describe it as a form of repentance. What do I mean by that? Simply, I decided that I wanted someone else to run my life, and I was willing to submit my life to a higher authority. In this case it was the drill instructors. It was at the end of the 12-week boot camp that I realized the drill instructors really wanted the best for us and they were busy trying to teach us how to survive in a brutal and hostile war zone. In order to do that we had to "co-labor" with them in the process or we would wash out and then come under another authority. That could mean you were "set back" (had to start over with another platoon) or got "brig time," "motivational platoon," or "dishonorable discharge." None of those were good options!

What is repentance? It is changing your thinking to line up with someone else's authority, or turning around and walking with another authority! Of course, none of us really understood that concept and it was a hard grinding to get in step with another authority other than our own.

Our Lord Jesus made it clear when He said, *"But seek first the kingdom of God and His righteousness, and all these things shall be added to you"* (Matthew 6:33).

Warriors, this is about being in a new kingdom! The allegiance to our own kingdom must come to an end so that we can come under the authority of a new king, and His name is Jesus! No one can force you to change kingdoms; it is a choice that you must make. However, the "Good News" is that our Father God and the Lord Jesus are lovingly recruiting you! They have sent the Holy Spirit to woo you as a man would pursue a bride he dearly loves and wants to train and mentor. (John 6:44, John 12:32). It is their desire to draw you into their kingdom and make you a vessel of honor. Paul, writing to Timothy, said, *"Therefore if anyone cleanses himself from the latter, he will be a vessel of honor, sanctified and useful for the Master, prepared for every good work"* (2 Timothy 2:21). We will look at honor in Chapter Eleven.

Scripture makes it very clear that our Father God wants everyone to be saved! *"For this is good and acceptable in the sight of God our Savior, who **desires all men to be saved** and to come to the knowledge of the truth"* (1 Timothy 2:3-4). Paul, again declaring this truth said, *"This is a faithful saying and worthy of all acceptance, that Christ Jesus came into the world **to save sinners**, of whom I am chief"* (1 Timothy 1:15). Then the Apostle Peter again made it abundantly clear that the will of God was that ALL come to repentance and salvation when he said: *"The Lord is not slack concerning His promise, as some count slackness, but is longsuffering toward us, **not willing that any should perish** but that **ALL** should come to repentance"* (2 Peter 3:9). The apostles Peter and Paul knew by experience that God was very patient, and that no sin was too big for the blood of Jesus!

Why did Paul claim to be the chief of sinners? Wasn't he a religious man? The fact is that he was not only religious, but was a leading Pharisee and was responsible for the imprisonment and torment of many Christians, both men and women. He was a religious zealot, a chief persecutor who had stood by, and witnessed the stoning of the first Christian martyr, Stephen. (Philippians 3:4-6, Acts 7:57-60 & 8:1-3)

It was only after his conversion that Saul became Paul and realized what terrible, inhumane things he had done—thus he knew he was a sinner saved by grace through repentance and the precious gift of God—not works of the law or flesh that he had learned as a Pharisee.

Let's look at the story of Saul's experience he had on the Damascus Road that led him to become a vessel of honor through his encounter and acceptance of a new king. Yes, King Jesus! The King of Kings and the Lord of Lords!

"All this time Saul was breathing down the necks of the Master's disciples, out for the kill. He went to the chief priest and got arrest warrants to take to the meeting places in

15

Damascus so that if he found anyone there belonging to the Way, whether men or women, he could arrest them and bring them to Jerusalem.

He set off. When he got to the outskirts of Damascus, he was suddenly dazed by a blinding flash of light. As he fell to the ground, he heard a voice: "Saul, Saul, why are you out to get me?"

He said, "Who are you, Master?"

"I am Jesus, the one you're hunting down. I want you to get up and enter the city. In the city you will be told what to do next."

His companions stood there dumbstruck—they could hear the sound, but couldn't see anyone—while Saul, picking himself up off the ground, found himself stone blind. They had to take him by the hand and lead him into Damascus. He continued blind for three days. He ate nothing, drank nothing.

There was a disciple in Damascus by the name of Ananias. The Master spoke to him in a vision: "Ananias."

"Yes Master?" He answered.

"Get up and go over to Straight Avenue. Ask at the house of Judas for a man from Tarsus. His name is Saul. He's there praying. He has just had a dream in which he saw a man named Ananias enter the house and lay hands on him so he could see again."

Ananias protested, "Master, you can't be serious. Everybody's talking about this man and the terrible things that he's been doing, his reign of terror against your people in Jerusalem! And now he's shown up here with papers from the Chief Priest that give him license to do the same to us."

But the Master said, "Don't argue. Go! I have picked him

16

as my personal representative to Gentiles and kings and Jews. And now I'm about to show him what he is in for—the hard suffering that goes with this job."

So Ananias went and found the house, placed his hands on blind Saul, and said, "Brother Saul, the Master sent me, the same Jesus you saw on the way here. He sent me so you could see again and be filled with the Holy Spirit." No sooner were the words out of his mouth than something like scales fell from Saul's eyes—he could see again! He got to his feet, was baptized, and sat down with them to a hearty meal" (Acts 9:1-19 The Message).

Wow, Saul went from being a religious terrorist (still have them today), to Paul, a leading apostolic minister of the Christian faith! I don't know about you, but I am glad that the bible is full of stories of men and women who had serious problems, sins, or issues, yet because of God's great love they made a decision to quit walking in their own way and turn around to walk in HIS way. That, beloved, is repentance!

You see, God is building an army and He knows that there will only be volunteers in His army. I shudder to consider the multitudes that warm church pews and believe that they are doing alright because at some point in time they went forward to an altar and prayed a sinner's prayer. Well, that is certainly a good beginning, but a beginning is all it is! God desires to have a people that will represent (or re-present) Him and reveal His glory to desperate and dying individuals and nations. That means we have to have a new King and be living in a new kingdom. **Taking and occupying the Kingdom is not a spectator sport, but rather hand to hand combat, and we must be trained to be effective.**

Two days after arriving at Parris Island the senior DI #2addressed us and asked, "Does anyone want to back out of your commitment and enlistment in the Marine Corps? Maybe you have decided that this is more than you bargained for, or maybe you are homesick and want to rethink your decision to become a Marine. If so, step forward now for this is your last and final chance. After today there is no turning back!"

What a joke! I knew that the DI's were playing some kind of game, for there was no turning back or having your enlistment voided. Well, one of the guys who was there because of a court order stepped forward and loudly proclaimed with cocky confidence, "I want my enlistment voided, I have changed my mind." Another big mistake! They told him to go to the back room and they would be with him in a few minutes to fill out the paper work.

So this cocky clown stepped out into the middle of the squad bay (we were only allowed to walk behind the bunks —never in the middle of the squad bay) and started sauntering toward the back room.

Well, at that time they had what was described as a "prayer meeting" with this fellow, and believe me, they were not praying. He received what was known as a "thumping" and proceeded to do hundreds of push ups and sit ups. He was then given a laundry bag of blank paper and for the next week he carried it around everywhere he went, including the head (toilet). Just imagine having that bag with you all the time. He had it with him when he got up in the morning, when he made our two-mile morning run, when he went to meals, when he cleaned the barracks, when he did morning drill and exercises, when he washed his clothes, when he shined his boots, when he cleaned his weapons, even when he went to the shower and bathroom! Everywhere he went, the bag went, and finally at lights out he slept with it! The bag was not heavy, but bulky, about the size of a big pillow. They explained that it was a symbol of his enlistment and that the only way he was going to get rid of it was to fall in love with it, therefore he had to have it with him all the time. Of course, everyone knew that you cannot void your enlistment; you are going to serve your time in one of two ways. The easy way or the hard way, the decision was up to the recruit. After a week he got the message and asked to be re-instated in the platoon, at which point he was allowed to discard the bag! He was beginning to get the message that if you want to get along in the kingdom, then you better learn how the kingdom functions. Incidentally, that recruit went on to become a leader in the platoon after he gave his heart to the discipline and training.

A stain on the evangelical church is that it has been made too easy to come into the kingdom! What do I mean by that? Simply this... Jesus said *"If any one wishes to come after Me, let him deny himself, and take up his cross and follow me. For whoever wished to save his life shall lose it: but whoever loses his life for My sake shall find it. For what will a man be profited, if he gains the whole world, and forfeits his soul? Or what will a man give in exchange for his soul? For the Son of Man is going to come in the glory of His Father and His angels; and will recompense every man according to his deeds"* (Matthew 16:24-27 NAS).

Too often the gospel invitation is presented as nothing more than a form of fire insurance. This leaves out the important truth that to be converted you must turn from your way and follow His way! This can only be done by taking on a new master and His name is Jesus! This always involves far more than just "asking Jesus into your heart." It involves a total commitment to walk with the King and follow in His footsteps, not your own!

A common error that is preached (it is really heresy) is that all you have to do to be saved is believe. Well, you certainly must believe, but you must also cooperate with the Spirit of God and go on to follow the Lord. Jesus made it very clear that we are to *"Bring forth fruit that is consistent with repentance—let your lives prove your change of heart"* (Matthew 3:8 AMP). I don't think I would be stretching it to translate it like this, "Prove or reveal that you have changed kingdoms!" If you have made Jesus your Lord and King, then your life will be changing—not all at once—but it will be changing!

The Cost of Following the King

I recently read that in China the evangelist makes it very difficult for you to make a decision for Christ as the evangelist explains over and over that this decision to follow Jesus could easily **cost your life**! The evangelist knows he has a spiritual responsibility to not "sugar coat" the gospel message, but to tell you plainly that walking with Jesus can cost you your life. He also knows that this earthly life is temporal and life with Jesus is eternal. Therefore, there is no comparison. Choose to walk with the King!

The fruit in China right now is almost unbelievable as 70,000 people per week are coming to Christ and being born again! Yes, that number is 70,000 per week! That is over 3.5 million people annually! Yes, Jesus is alive and well on planet earth!

This is even more remarkable when you understand that this is happening mostly in underground churches and the persecution is terrible. It is said that every Christian leader in China has spent at least three years "hard time" in prison and many are there for 20 years.[#3]Yet the gospel is growing and the grace of God is expanding faster and faster and all this without the advantage of high tech assistance.

In many parts of the world today it requires the heart of a warrior just to survive. Just as in the days of the early church, persecution is rampant and Christians are being martyred by the thousands, in fact the number is in the millions. It is common knowledge (although not talked about) that there are over 200 million Christians facing persecution on a daily basis and 60% of those are children. Between 12,000 and 17,000 Christians are being martyred each month... Yes, each month! And many more are being imprisoned, brutalized, and separated from family, tortured, threatened, and sold as slaves.[4] These figures are hard for Americans to believe as we live in such a privileged society and often the greatest offense we have to deal with is someone getting on our nerves or cutting us off in traffic!

But our Father is bringing forth an army of trained men and women who have made Jesus not only their King, but also the Captain of their salvation; and they are called, trained and destined to set creation free!

In Jesus' prayer to the Father in John 17 he said: *"As You sent me into the world, I also have sent them into the world"* (John 17:18). Now in First John we see clearly what the Father had in mind for Jesus. *"For this purpose the son of God was manifested, that He might destroy the works of the devil"* (I John 3:8B). So what is Jesus sending us forth to do? Simple: To destroy the works of the devil by *"preaching the gospel to the poor, heal the brokenhearted, proclaim liberty to the captives, recovery of sight to the blind, to set at liberty those who are oppressed and to proclaim the acceptable year of the Lord"* (Luke 4:18-19). I believe that a favorite scripture for the church in these last days will be *"Now, Lord, look on their (those that want to persecute and martyr us) threats, and grant to your servants that with all boldness they may speak your word, by stretching out your hand to heal, and that signs and wonders may be done through the name of your holy Servant Jesus"* (Acts 4:29-30).

Yes Lord! Move in grace and power to save, heal, and deliver all those that come against you even as you did for Saul!

Martyrs

Statistics[4] show that Christians are being martyred in Indonesia, Bangladesh, India[5], Nigeria, East Timor, Cuba, Viet ⁎ Nam, China, the former Soviet Republics, Saudi Arabia, Iran, Iraq, and other Muslim countries. In the last 2,000 years about 70 million have given their lives for the Lord Jesus and of those 70 million it is estimated that 45 million of these martyrs or 65% have died in the last century!

We know that eleven of the twelve original apostles were martyred:[6]

1. Andrew – crucified

2. Bartholomew – beaten, then crucified

3. James, son of Alphaeus – stoned to death

4. James, son of Zebedee – beheaded

5. John – exiled for his faith: died of old age

6. Judas (not Iscariot) – stoned to death

7. Matthew – speared to death

8. Peter – crucified upside down

9. Philip – crucified

10. Simon – crucified

11. Thomas – speared to death

12. Matthias – stoned to death

These men were willing to lay down their lives because they had "counted the cost" and to live or die for the Lord Jesus was nothing but gain for them. They had seen Jesus be crucified, dead, and buried, and they saw and knew Him after the resurrection. They knew that His resurrected life lived in them and no cost was too great to live or die for Him. The apostle Paul, who was later martyred, wrote *"I prefer rather to be absent from the body and to be at home with the Lord"* (2 Corinthians 5:8 NAS). Now that is faith! Paul had it because he had lived it and knew that it was truth. It was not a theological theory; it was truth, eternal truth!

I am not one who thinks we should live in fear of what may happen, but rather I believe that we need to develop such an intimacy with the Father, Son and Holy Spirit that we are at perfect peace with whatever comes our way. At the same time, we must not be foolish and not be prepared just because we feel secure in our environment. The story of the virgins is too important to miss! Remember now, we are talking about the kingdom and the King!

"Then the kingdom of heaven shall be likened to ten virgins who took their lamps and went to meet the bridegroom.

1- *Five of them were foolish—thoughtless, without fore thought; and five were wise—sensible, intelligent and prudent.*

2- *For when the foolish took their lamps, they did not take any (extra) oil with them;*

3- *But the wise took flasks of oil along with them (also) with their lamps.*

4- *While the bridegroom lingered and was slow in coming, they all began nodding their heads and fell asleep.*

5- *But at midnight there was a shout, Behold, the bridegroom! Go out to meet him!*

6- *Then all those virgins got up and put their own*

lamps in order.

7- And the foolish said to the wise, Give us some of your oil, for our lamps are going out.

8- But the wise replied, There will not be enough for us and for you; go instead to the dealers and buy for yourselves.

9- But while they were gone away to buy, the bride groom came, and those who were prepared went in with him to the marriage feast; and the door was shut.

10- Later the other virgins also came, and said, Lord, Lord, open the door to us!

11- But He replied, I solemnly declare to you, I do not know you—I am not acquainted with you.

12- Watch therefore—give strict attention and be cautious and active—for you know neither the day nor the hour when the Son of Man will come" (Matthew 25:1-13 AMP).

Beloved, we need to be very clear here, the issue is about intimacy with the Lord! The reason the martyrs willingly gave their lives for the King was because they loved Him and had become so intimate with Him that they were at peace in His presence! His presence was everything to them and they knew that to be absent from the body is to be present with the Lord in a deeper measure. They have paid the price to buy the oil—which is the anointing—and that is all that matters to them. He knows them and they know Him! Clear and Simple!

Warriors have established in their hearts that they are willing to pay the ultimate price for freedom. There are many members in the body of Christ that are willing to do the same—give their life—not only for the Lord, but also for the testimony and the glory that the Lord is placing in His body!

As a Marine veteran of the Viet ✳ Nam era, [7] I remember well the saying: *"All gave some... Some gave all!"* That was true for over 58,000 warriors!

A Band of Brothers

"He which hath no stomach to this fight let him depart. But we in it shall be remembered. We few, we happy few, we band of brothers!! For he today, that sheds his blood with me, shall always be my brother." [8]

Church! Are we going to be that **"Band of Brothers"** that will commit our lives to the King of Kings and the Lord of Lords—to be trained as warriors to stand in the gap in this hour for His Kingdom which is everlasting?

Will we unite and stand as a nation of warriors that will stand for justice, the widows, the hungry, the oppressed, the fatherless, and all those without hope in this desolate generation?

Will we answer the high calling in Christ Jesus to set the captive free and have a "Warrior's Walk" with Jesus? Will we walk as He walked for the purpose that we might participate with Him in *"destroying the works of the devil"* (1 John 3:8)?

Warriors run to the sound of battle, not away from it. And they make sure they are as prepared as possible before they are given their marching orders.

There can be no victory without a battle, and lack of preparation is a certain receipt for disaster. Do you hear the trumpet sound calling you to prepare? Have you **"Counted the Cost?"**

In the next chapter, let's look at some training principles that are just as important to a spiritual "Warrior" as they are to a combat Marine.

Endnotes: Chapter One

#1- I highly recommend that you read Bill Johnson's book "When Heaven Invades Earth" published by Destiny Image (www.destinyimage. com) for a deeper understanding of the move of God that is happening in the hour! There are a vast number of Christians seeing the miracles, signs, and wonders revealing the love and grace of the Father, Son and Holy Spirit. You, too, can be a part of this powerful and exciting move that is happening (even in the United States) as we believe that God has not changed, but is the same today as He was yesterday—meaning He is still performing miracles, signs, and wonders for His glory!

#2- Each platoon in Marine basic training has three drill instructors. One is the senior drill instructor and the other two are referred to as junior drill instructors. They usually rank anywhere from corporal E-4 to Staff Sergeant E-6. Occasionally substitute drill instructors will fill in for one of the others. Also in the command structure there was a Battalion Commander (Lt. Colonel), a Company Commander (Captain), a Series Commander(1st Lt), a chief drill instructor (Gy Sgt) and a series Gunnery Sergeant (Gy Sgt).

Gy. Sgt. Jettie Rivers, our series Gunnery Sergeant was killed by rocket and mortar fire during a battle in the Quang Tri province of South Viet Nam. He was killed June 6, 1967, almost four years after I first met him. For his valor while saving lives he was awarded the second highest award, The Navy Cross! Thank You Gunny for being faithful to us and to our country! We were better and safer because of you!

#3- James Rutz has written a powerful well researched and documented book called "Mega Shift" (www.megashift.org). This is a must read to understand the "igniting spiritual power" that is sweeping the earth in this hour. This book is available from Empowerment Press, 102 South Tejon Street, Suite 1100, Colorado Springs, Colorado 80903; phone 719-578-3359.

#4- The ZENIT.org News Agency was reporting conclusions of a new book "The New Persecuted" by journalist Antonio Socci.

#5- John Shergur, a minister with Restoring Hearts Ministries has traveled and ministered in India and has first hand knowledge of the persecution.

#6- Sources: "Fox's Book of Martyrs", written by John Fox, 1516-1587. Edited by William Byron Forbush. Original copyright 1926.

#7- I enlisted in the Marine Corps on September 10, 1963 and was at Parris Island within ten days. I was honorably discharged as an E5 Sergeant (three stripes) six years later in Sept. 1969. Most of time was spent assigned to an Artillery Battery and my last duty was the Commanding Officer's driver and assistant. We were constantly being trained and retrained to be ready for combat and were certain that at any time our unit would be called up to go "in country, the country of living hell" referring to Viet ✴ Nam. Either by God's grace or some other miracle we were never called up. Of course in the 60's the US actually had many more fighting men and women prepared for war and they were concerned to put all their troops in one combat theatre. They knew that other problems could manifest at any time throughout the world.

#8- Quote by William Shakespeare 1564-1616, from his play "Henry V", Act IV. Scene 3.

"Suffer hardship with me, as a good soldier of Jesus Christ.

No soldier in active service entangles himself in the affairs of everyday life, so that he may please the one who enlisted him as a soldier

And if anyone competes as an athlete, he does not win the prize unless he competes according to the rules."

2 Timothy 2:3-5 NAS

Chapter Two

One New Man
Our training begins

Sergeant Major Bill Paxton, a famous Marine who was known as part of the Old Breed has been quoted as saying: **"If you don't get discipline in boot camp, it's too late to get it in combat. It's just technique and discipline. The more we sweat in peacetime, the less we bleed in war. No Marine ever died in his own sweat."** [1]

No doubt every recruit that landed on Parris Island with me had their own ideas about what was going to happen and how that would look and feel to them. But the Marine Corps had a definite plan; and that plan was to take a group of individuals and mold them into a precise, dedicated, motivated unit that would learn to move as one new man!

The Marine Drill Instructors who had been assigned to our platoon had been well trained and their training was much tougher than ours. In fact, the wash out rate in drill instructors school was much higher than the wash out rate in recruit training.

Church, today our Warrior leaders in this hour need to be the best trained and equipped in order to lead us into the fray of battle. Many dear folks have followed leaders that have not given themselves to the battle. Many of these same dear folks have become the walking wounded, while some have even given up the fight! This must stop!

I mentioned in the introduction that Ephesians 4:11-16 spoke of the five fold ministry taking the church to a place where they were fit for the work of the ministry and that we should no longer be children.

In my experience the church is still filled with people concerned about their own kingdom, rather than the Kingdom of God. Well, the DI's had been well trained to work and bring over 80 people together, each with their own ideas, patterns of behavior, honor codes, and life programming and mold them into an entirely new way of thinking.

How could they do that?

Immediate obedience

Immediate obedience is the toughest, but the most critical of disciplines that every Marine and that every Christian must learn!

In boot camp you have three DI's and you learn to know their voices within a couple of days; but learning to hear the voice of the Lord is often more difficult. The reason we don't hear the voice of the Lord as quickly is because we don't spend the time with Him to get to know His voice. You learn to hear the voice of your DI's because you spend 24 hours a day for thirteen straight weeks. That is over 2200 hours of intense personal hearing and obeying. And obey you did, unless you were rebellious! You say, but what about sleeping? They would wake you up at various hours and demand that you be combat ready almost immediately, because they knew alertness and readiness were necessities in battle.

Remember our Lord Jesus asked His disciples to watch and pray with Him? They couldn't do it and He explained that the reason they couldn't was because *"the spirit indeed is willing, but the flesh is weak."* [2]

The story goes like this: *"Then Jesus went with them to a garden called Gethsemane and told His disciples, 'Stay here while I go over there and pray.' Taking along Peter and the two sons of Zebedee, he plunged into an agonizing sorrow.*

Then He said 'This sorrow is crushing my life out. Stay here and keep vigil (watch) with me'.

Going a little ahead, He fell on His face praying, 'My Father, if there is any way, get me out of this. But please, not what I want. You, what do You want?'

When He came back to His disciples, He found them sound asleep. He said to Peter, "Can't you stick it out with me a single hour? **Stay alert; be in prayer so you don't wander into temptation without even knowing you're in danger.** *There is part of you that is eager, ready for anything in God. But there's another part that's as lazy as an old dog sleeping by the fire."*

He then left them a second time. Again He prayed, "My Father, if there is no other way than this, drinking this cup to the dregs, I'm ready. Do it your way."

When He came back, He again found them sound asleep. They simply couldn't keep their eyes open. This time He let them sleep on, and went back a third time to pray going over the same ground one last time.

When He came back the next time, He said, "Are you going to sleep on and make a night of it? My time is up, the Son of Man is about to be handed over to the hands of sinners. Get up! Let's get going! My betrayer is here" (Matthew 26:36-46 MSG).

For me the most frightening experience I had while at Parris Island was a night I was on guard duty. My duty was a two hour shift during the early morning hours. I was assigned to patrol around the barracks and the mess hall. The problem was that behind the mess hall there was a small bench and I decided to sit down for a few minutes. I fell asleep sitting there! Something startled me and I jumped to my feet and took a couple steps just as the officer of the day came around the corner! Saved by the skin of two steps!

You say, well what is the big deal? Well the big deal is that if he had caught me snoozing I could have been sent to the motivation platoon (I will explain the motivation platoon later)! It was very serious business as they knew that in combat many men and women had been killed because someone could not stay awake!

"Stay Alert; be in prayer so you don't wander into temptation without even knowing you're in danger" (Matthew 26:41 MSG).

We must learn to stay alert and pay attention to hear the voice of the Lord! It is a big deal and if we don't hear His voice we can easily be led astray and take wrong turns in life. Remember, that our Father God has a plan [#3] for our life that is both glorious and wonderful, but we have to hear Him speak to us in order to walk in His ordained path. It is not complicated, but it does require listening! Jesus made it clear when He said: *"My sheep hear My voice, and I know them, and they follow me"* (John 10:27).

Often something drastic has to happen to get our attention in order to hear clearly and immediately obey.

A recruit shot?

A platoon in my company had this experience that immediately brought them to instant obedience!

On the first day the recruits have to run from the receiving area to the barracks. It was a distance of over a mile and they were carrying all of their new gear. The gear probably weighed about 60 pounds, and was real bulky. They had to run up the steps to the third floor of the barracks. There was one recruit that had been lagging way behind and exhibiting a sorry attitude. One of the DI's had been running right with him yelling at him and trying to help him along. When all the rest of the recruits had made it into the barracks and had been lined up in front of the bunks this last recruit finally made it to the top of the stairs and was almost in the door when he stopped and cursed the DI. Yeah, he just cursed the DI right to his face! Everyone was shocked into total silence waiting to see what was going to happen, but nothing could prepare them for what did happen! The DI was already in the door and the recruit was framed in the doorway when he cursed the DI!

Then it happened! It was so sudden and so violent that the recruits were not even sure what they had seen. They certainly could barely believe what they had seen.

Well, what had they seen? They saw the DI draw a .45 caliber pistol and fire point blank into the recruit's chest! The recruit grabbed his bloody chest and fell back out the door, down the steps, not to be seen again! They didn't even know his name!

At that point, the DI calmly turned to the platoon and proclaimed **"That's what happens to recruits that are insolent, rebellious, and lazy and won't listen to commands!" Anyone care to argue about it? Don't make me tell you anything more than once and obey immediately! You are in the Marine Corps now and we sometimes do it the hard way. You make the choice... the hard way or the easy way! It is up to you! It is not complicated, instant obedience or instant regret."**

Needless to say that was one of the best disciplined platoons that had ever been through basic training at Parris Island!

The truth did not come out till weeks later when one of the recruits saw the recruit that had supposedly been shot at the mess hall. It was then that he realized that the dead recruit was actually a DI that had only been playing a starring role in a one act play!

I am sure that play was not standard operating procedure, but it illustrates the dynamic of obedience.

What does it mean to hear?

It means that you will be walking in your **God ordained destiny** and manifesting the glory of God in the earth. To not hear God is to miss completely God's destiny that He has for you!

How would you respond if you were a teenage gal and an angel named Gabriel showed up and told you that you were going to become pregnant and that baby was going to be the given throne of David and a kingdom that would never end? Yeah right! Not exactly an everyday occurrence! Now Mary had been to the sex education classes at the synagogue and she knew that the only way to get pregnant was to be intimate with a man, thereby resulting in conception. But no, that was not what this angel Gabriel was talking about! Gabriel told her that the Holy Spirit would come upon her and she would get pregnant. She argued and said "but I have never slept with my fiancée Joseph or any other man!" You see Mary was still **hearing and thinking in the natural**, and what Gabriel was talking about was completely supernatural. Totally outside the box of Mary's thinking or anyone else's for that matter!

But **hear and obey** is exactly what Mary did, for she replied to Gabriel *"Yes I see it all now: I'm the Lord's maid, ready to serve. Let it be with me just as you say"* (Luke 1:38 MSG).

How many times have we read this story without realizing the tremendous cost that both Mary and Joseph paid to

hear the word and obey it? Can you imagine the slurs and taunts that they were tormented with all over town and in the synagogue as well? The words spoken in public were nothing compared to the words that were spoken behind their back, and you know they heard those as well.

In the gospel of Matthew Chapter 1:19-21 we see that Joseph was a just man and he was going to hide Mary away (since she must be an immoral woman) until the birth, but the angel of the Lord appeared to him in a dream saying *"Joseph, son of David, do not be afraid to take to you Mary your wife, for that which is conceived in her is of the Holy Spirit. And she will bring forth a Son, and you shall call his name Jesus, for he will save His people from their sins."* Then in verse 24-25 it says: *"Then Joseph being aroused from sleep, **did as the angel of the Lord commanded him** and took to him his wife, and did not know her (no intimate sexual relations) until she had brought forth her firstborn Son. And he called His name Jesus."* After Joseph heard the word of the Lord through the angel **he obeyed**!

Hearing means obedience!

Let's look at some life changing scriptures that reveal the deep truth that **hearing is obeying**. Volumes have been written about hearing and obeying the word, but I believe that these three scriptures bring the truth into a glorious light that is undeniable.

The First scripture Romans 5:19 taken from the NKJ is: *"For as by one man's disobedience (Strong's #3876) many were made sinners, so also by one Man's obedience (Strong's #5218) many will be made righteous."*

Now when we look at the original Greek words and the deeper meaning it is very telling.

The word **disobedience** (Strong's #3876) says: **"That in the strictest sense a failing to hear, or hearing amiss, with the notion of active disobedience which follows this inattentive or careless hearing."** Yikes! Do you see it? Disobedience and failing to hear, hearing amiss, inattentive or careless hearing are one and the same! When we hear the living word of the living God we are responsible to obey and act according to that word. Now the word **obedience** (Strong's #5218) is also linked to hearing as it literally means: **"to hearken, to listen to something, to obey."** Yikes again! Do you see it? Obedience requires that you hear first the living word of the living God and that you hearken, listen and obey.

The second scripture Hebrews 2:1-3 taken from the NKJ is: *"Therefore we must give the more earnest heed to the things we have heard, lest we drift away. For if the word spoken through angels proved steadfast, and every transgression and disobedience **(Strong's #3876—"in the strictest sense a failing to hear or hearing amiss, with the notion of active disobedience which follows the inattentive or careless hearing")** received a just recompense of reward. How shall we escape if we neglect so great a salvation, which at the first began to be spoken by the Lord, and was confirmed to us by those who heard Him?"*

Because we are talking about *"The Warrior's Walk"* the third scripture also taken from the NKJ is vital for us to comprehend. For without this comprehension there will be a shaky walk at best, and many important battles will be compromised or lost completely.

2 Corinthians 10:4-5 says: *"For the weapons of our warfare are not carnal but mighty in God for pulling down strongholds, casting down imaginations and every high thing that exalts itself against the knowledge of God, bringing every thought into captivity to the obedience **(Strong's #5218:***

"to hearken, to listen to something, to obey") of Christ."

Beloved, if we are going into battle with the Captain of our Salvation we better know how to hear His voice and distinguish His voice from all others. For only His voice speaks the words of life! All other voices will surely try and derail you and shipwreck you. Only the King of Kings, the Captain of our Salvation has the words of life that will set us free and move us into His destiny that He desires for us to walk in. We must be trained to listen, and having listened, then we must obey! Truly your ears are the key to walking in your God appointed destiny. He will not force you—He will only speak to you the words of life saying things such as: *"This is the way, walk in it"* (Isaiah 30:21b).

It is pretty simple. If you don't hear His word, then you won't know the way to walk!

Did you hear His voice?

Jesus said *"My sheep **hear** my voice, and I know them, and they follow me"* (John 10:27). Who **heard** His voice?

We have already looked at Joseph and Mary and how they **heard** the word of the Lord through the angel.

Peter, Andrew, James and John all **heard** those famous words *"Follow me and I will make you fishers of men"* (Matthew 4:18-21). History is filled with exciting stories of other men and women who heard those same words and followed!

The leper came down from the mountains and asked this key question of Jesus "Lord, if You are willing, You can make me clean." Then the leper **heard** these words as Jesus touched him, *"I am willing; be cleansed"* (Matthew 8:1-3). As tragic as it is, many today are not willing to come to Jesus and ask that same question, Lord, if you are willing! They have bought into the lie of the religious naysayer that has said that Jesus does not heal any more. Saints, if you are **hearing** this word, then **GO** and tell the creation that is desperate for His touch—many of them are sitting next to you in a church pew, at a PTA meeting, a sports event or standing in the grocery store line! Tell them that Jesus is the same today as He was when He walked the earth 2,000 years ago. Listen for His voice – He will tell you what to do.

Matthew the tax collector **heard** those precious words "Follow Me" which he did until the day he was speared to death for his faith in the King of Kings. He knew what the cost might be and he gladly paid it.

We learn to hear by 'neglect'!

Some years ago I saw an interview of a 12-year-old girl who was playing the violin for some major symphonies. The interviewer asked her how she had developed into such an extraordinary violinist at such a young age. Her answer had a profound impact on me, for she said "I have achieved this level through neglect!" The interviewer was taken back by her answer and said "How is that possible to get to that level through neglect? I don't understand." The young girl smiled brightly and said, "It is really quite easy, I have neglected all else but the violin which I dearly love. I don't have time for video games, television, movies, entertainment – those things are just a distraction from what I love; so I chose to neglect them!" Wow! Was I convicted!

What was she neglecting? Everything, but her love and devotion for the violin; because all the other things that most kids like were only a distraction for her. You see she did not feel that she was being deprived in any way. In fact she was delighted because she was getting what she wanted, and that was her passion for music and the violin in particular.

We should ask ourselves the question: "What would the

world and our life be like if we ignored all but the King of Kings and His kingdom, and what He wanted us to say and do?"

*"Faith comes by **hearing**, and **hearing** by the word of God"* (Romans 10:17). We have to be trained to hear the word of God and to hear His voice. We do that by coming into His presence and having sweet communion with Him!

Those that failed to hear or heard amiss!

Okay, let's look at some folks who **did not hear, heard amiss or were careless, inattentive resulting in active disobedience**. They not only missed their destiny, but caused major problems.

- I suppose that we have to start with Adam and Eve. They sure got things in tornadic turmoil when they **heard** the voice of God, but decided to listen and give ear to the enemy's voice. It cost them dearly and it cost us dearly as well. Wow, talk about missing your destiny! Praise God He was prepared for the *fall* and provided us with a Savior! (Genesis 2:16-17, 3:1-24).

- *"That same day Nadab and Abihu, Aaron's sons, took their censors, put hot coals and incense in them, and offered **strange fire** to God – something God had not commanded.* They heard amiss—Fire blazed out from God and consumed them—they died in God's presence. (Leviticus 10:1-2 MSG). These boys were careless about their office as priests and it not only cost them their destiny, but their lives! Hearing God is serious business!

- The *"Suddenly"* that Aaron and Miriam **heard** in Numbers 12:4 was not a comforting voice! God was getting ready to demonstrate that He is serious when He says

"Don't speak evil of dignitaries" (2 Peter 2:10) and *"Let no corrupt communication proceed out of you mouth and let all evil speaking be put away from you"* (Ephesians 4:29-32). You see they had criticized Moses regarding the choice of his wife and God had demonstrated how He felt about it by laying a little 'leprosy' on Miriam. What a price to pay for running that mouth in criticism! She learned the hard lesson that *"death and life are in the power of the tongue"* (Proverbs 18:21)! Now the good news is that they repented of their foolishness and appealed to Moses who prayed for them. And after seven days outside the camp Miriam was healed and restored! (Number 12:1-16)

- The 10 spies had **heard** the clear word of the Lord that He was giving them a land flowing with milk and honey but they **heard amiss** and missed out on the promise land. In a nutshell they just plain refused to believe and trust God to do what looked like the impossible, **failing to hear** that our God is the God of the impossible! (Number 13:1-33)

It is a sad commentary that all the children of Israel who were delivered out of Egypt died in the wilderness because of a **failure to hear**, resulting in constant complaining, murmuring and disobedience. They were mad at God and at His servants (their **self determination** was more important than their destiny) and refused to enter into the destiny that God had ordained and called them to. The whole generation that came out of Egypt died in the wilderness except for Joshua and Caleb. It was the generation that was born in the wilderness that after 40 years finally entered in. The New Testament reality is evident in Hebrews Chapters 3 and 4. We see there that He said, *"Today if you will **hear** His voice, Do not harden your hearts as in the rebellion."* He then repeats it two more times for good measure! *"Today if you will hear His voice! Today if you will hear His voice!* (Hebrews 3:7-8,

15 & Chapter 4:7). Three times He says the same thing—He is trying to get our attention! Are we listening?

Saints: who heard, obeyed and walked in their destiny

Okay, let's look at some folks who heard the word knew the voice of God and obeyed His voice resulting in not only their destiny being changed, but history was changed as well.

- We have already seen that Mary and Joseph's life was radically changed **hearing** the voice of God being spoken through the angel. (Luke 1:38, Matthew 1:19-25)

- Abraham answered and said *"Here I am"* and at that point of **hearing**—God tested Abraham with the thing he loved the most which was his son Isaac. Abraham passed the test and fulfilled the destiny of being the father of multitudes. Further tests resulted in Abraham being called the "friend of God" because of **hearing** and obeying (Genesis Chapter 22, James 2:23, Isaiah 41:8, Romans Chapter 4).

- During a third heaven experience Jacob saw the Lord and the angels ascending and descending from heaven to earth and from earth to heaven and **heard** the Lord say *"I will not leave you until I have done what I have spoken to you"* (Genesis 28:10-22).

- The Angel of the Lord appeared to Moses in a flame of fire from the midst of a bush and when Moses turned aside to look at it he heard God say, *"Moses. Moses!"* And then the life changing words: *"I AM WHO I AM! I am sending you to set my people free of the captivity of Egypt and you will change the destiny of My people"* (my paraphrase). Exodus chapter three.

• Caleb clearly **heard** the promise in Numbers 13:2 of what the Lord had spoken regarding taking the Promised Land and he stood up to the 10 disbelieving, faithless spies who saw the giants and said that it was impossible to conquer. They all died in their fear, but Caleb along with Joshua entered into the glory. Only Joshua and Caleb **heard** the Lord and entered into their destiny!

• The Lord spoke and Joshua **heard** that God was giving them the land, to be strong and of good courage, for the Lord your God is with you wherever you go. (Joshua 1:1-9). Joshua took those words he heard and walked as a warrior into the promise land, therefore fulfilling his destiny as well as Israel's. That beloved is *"The Warrior's Walk."*

• In Judges 6:1-10 we see that the children of Israel **"Did not obey God's voice"** and for that reason they were under great oppression from their enemies. Then the Angel of the Lord came and sat with Gideon who was of the weakest clan and the least or puniest in his father's house. In other words, this Gideon was a wimp! But those are the very people that God loves to use, because they know that they cannot do it without His divine help! Then Gideon **heard** the words of promise from the Lord and delivered the children of Israel from the hand of the enemy (Judges 6, 7, & 8).

• It took Samuel four tries, but Samuel **learned to hear** the voice of the Lord and having **learned to hear** he fulfilled his own destiny; and moved in power as the priest of God. It is important to note that Samuel first heard the voice of the Lord as he was ministering to the Lord. And his answer was *"Speak for your servant hears."* Beloved, intimacy with the Lord brings His voice into clarity. Can we do less than press in to hear

His voice? (1 Samuel 3:1-21)

• Okay, no study on hearing God would be complete without looking at Peter walking on the water! It is just too cool a story to leave out of the countless examples we could use. Yes, Peter walked on water! That defied all laws of gravity and nature, yet he did it because he **heard** the voice and the word of Jesus! The natural becomes supernatural when we **hear** His voice. Peter **heard** this word and it transformed the natural into the supernatural. The word was simply *"Come"* spoken to Peter after he asked Jesus if it was Him on the water. That simple word *"Come"* broke the barrier of the natural and put Peter into the supernatural and that same word will put us into the supernatural as well! Beloved, we are to live in the eternal realm which is supernatural! You say well what was the purpose of walking on the water? The reason is clear and it is to demonstrate that when we **hear and obey** His voice there is nothing too hard for us. Come on church, step out of your boat (comfort zone) and walk on the water with Jesus! That's what it will take to set creation free. The supernatural overcoming the natural!

Endnotes: Chapter Two

#1- Quote from Sergeant Major Bill Paxton found in "The Few & The Proud" by Larry Smith, published by W.W. Norton & Company, Inc. 500 Fifth Avenue, New York, NY 10110, copyright 2006.

#2- Only eternity will show the true value of prayer, but there is no doubt that prayer is what brings revival, maintains revival, changes individuals, changes churches, changes countries and transforms cultures.

Pastors Mahesh and Bonnie Chavda started a "Watch Service" over 12 years ago and they have met faithfully with the folks from All Nations Church every Friday night from 7:30pm to 6:00am. Their faithfulness has turned into a "prayer watch movement" that now has over 1,800 churches meeting to "Watch and Pray" on a weekly basis! For more information check out their website @ www.WatchoftheLord.com.

International House of Prayer began a 24 hours per day—365 days per year prayer in 1999 and is going even stronger today. An excerpt from their web site says: "A prayer meeting began which continues to this day, from dawn till dusk and throughout the watches of the night. Prayer and worship continues 24 hours a day, seven days per week. The prayer room is the heartbeat—the essence and the origin—of all that goes on at the International House of Prayer. May the fire on the altar never go out." Check out their web site for more teaching and information at www.ihop.org.

#3- *For I know the thoughts that I think toward you, says the Lord, thoughts of peace and not of evil, to give you a future and a hope*" (Jeremiah 29:11).

A hard reality of life is that no one lives only unto themselves—there are always other people that are affected by our choices and actions, whether they are good or bad.

I remember many times as a police chaplain talking to people who wanted to kill themselves and they would always say, "No one will care if I'm dead and gone!" Yet, in each of these situations there were always family and friends who are deeply affected and often distraught for life. No man is an island unto himself and that is particularly true with both the Marine Corps and all of the armed services and the body of Christ!

"God is not changing us to stay the same"

Tonda S. Payne

Chapter Three

Life was about to change

Remember that the Marine Corps recruiter told me that my life was about to change and that the change would be forever? Well, he wasn't kidding! A *"Warrior's Walk"* is about change, not only in the Marine Corps, but also in the army of God. My wife Tonda got the revelation years ago that **"God is not changing us to stay the same."** Sounds simple, but that is a profound revelation and I share it in almost every meeting, seminar or conference that I am involved in. The Christian life is always about change, and the reason the church in the western world is so stagnant is because they have such a resistance and aversion to change.

Think of a stagnant pool of water... pretty yucky... it is either dead or dying because there is no water going in or out. Jesus said that He could give us "living water" and that we would never thirst again. He also made it clear that *"God is not the God of the dead, but the God of the living"* (Luke 22:32B, Mark 12:27, Luke 20:38 NAS).

I can't tell you how many born again, spirit filled believers that I talk to who tell me they are bored, yes bored! My observation is that boredom comes because they are in a stagnant place—either in their own life or in their church life. Beloved, what we have been given—the living water—must be given away!

Now, when I went to Parris Island to be trained as a Marine I was not bored, but I was certainly stagnant. Because of that stagnation I was going in all the wrong directions. Parris Island changed my life and gave me new direction!

A New Focus

Prior to Parris Island my life was all about me and what I could get from it or out of it. That is where many Christians are today, looking for what they can get from God, instead of looking to be trained to glorify His name and reveal His purposes in the earth. Now that is a new focus and a focus worthy of giving our life for. Even in my military prep school training the emphasis was on what you could get out of life for yourself, be it a bigger house, better paying job, vacation homes and all sorts of assorted big boy toys. The millions who are suffering persecution in the world for following our Lord Jesus find it ludicrous that we are so concerned about things that have no eternal value. It is a true saying that "kingdom abundance is not measured in what we have, but rather in what we have given away!"

As I write this we are experiencing a severe drought in the Carolinas and people are becoming indignant that they are not allowed to water their luscious lawns when they want to. I wonder how indignant they will be if they have no water to drink? I believe that it is no accident that as we are experiencing a natural drought, that we are also experiencing a spiritual drought in so many places. God has an answer for us and all of the church if we will just heed His voice. He is trying to get our attention now so that in that hour we will be prepared for what is to come. How do we prepare? Well, we begin by coming to the water!

Come to the Waters

Isaiah said "Ho! Everyone who thirsts,
Come to the waters;
And you who have no money,
Come buy and eat.
Yes, come buy wine and milk
Without money and without price.
Why do you spend money
For what is not bread,
And your wages for what does not satisfy?
Listen Carefully to Me,
And eat what is good,
And let your soul delight itself in abundance."

Isaiah 55:1-2

Jesus is the living water and we must come to Him, not because we have to, but because we want to.

It is fascinating that God is moving in such power and grace in the world and many churches are filled with folks who have not got a clue what He is doing! Over the last number of years I have seen countless number of miracles, signs and wonders and yet many still either don't want to believe it or are afraid to believe it. Why? Because they are comfortable! And they are afraid to change which might make them uncomfortable, even if it means giving glory to God and walking in His miraculous power. Call it by any name you like, but the bottom line is that it is UNBELIEF! The enemy has truly blinded the eyes of multitudes. *"But even if the gospel is veiled, it is veiled to those who are perishing, whose minds the god of this age has blinded,* **who do not believe***, lest the light of the gospel of the glory of Christ, who is the image of God, should shine on them"* (2 Corinthians 4:3-4). Some might say that this scripture was written to unbelievers and I would agree with that, as many churches are filled with unbelievers, who profess to know God, but deny His power! They are holding to a form or tradition or cessationist [#1]type teaching, which is denying His power! What a tragedy!

But Hey! That is what we are fighting for and being trained for. If everything was perfect we could just fold up our tents and go watch the sunset.

"Receiving" and Shared Hardships

Life changes fast at Parris Island! Today I understand that a recruit spends a week at receiving, but we only spent about half a day. The transformation is now into full swing. It started when we got off the bus and it continued for 12 full weeks.

We had already learned how to bury sand fleas and how not to eat cigarettes and obviously they had our undivided attention, at least mine for sure.

We did not realize it but they were forcing us (burying sand fleas) to work together, whether we wanted to or not. We were learning to **complete each other and not compete with each other**[#2] and to move as one unit and not just as individuals. The individual training would come later, but now we needed to learn to work together. One of the ways that happens is when you experience the shared hardships together. That meant when one of us messed up, we all paid for it. Of course as you are paying for someone else's mistake you are getting stronger since you are doing pushups and running more together. Sure did not make sense then, but as I looked back I saw the wisdom of what they were doing and realized that God is doing the same with His church in this hour.

You see those believers in China that have to hide to fellowship together have drawn close together in the shared hardships of persecutions. Petty things like how long the meetings last, too tired to go, or don't need anything else spiritually reveal that we are not a desperate people that are hungry for God. God loves it when His people are hungry and God cannot help but respond to our hunger!

Jesus said *"Blessed are those who hunger and thirst for righteousness, for they shall be filled"* (Matthew 5:6).

He also said *"I am the bread of life.* **He who comes to Me** *shall never hunger, and he who believes in me shall never thirst"* (John 6:35).

Beloved, it takes hunger to get in His presence and receive the daily manna that He is trying to give us, but it is well worth the diligence required.

During seminars and conferences around the country I am fascinated by the people that come to the meetings and the ones that don't. If people come during a week night (or any other time except Sunday morning) it is usually because they are hungry. They long to know "the more" of what God may be doing and they will pay a price to get "the more".

I remember being in a big church that had a large staff and I was surprised that more of the staff was not present at the meetings. The pastor shared with me that some of them thought that they had all the understanding they needed about restoration and healing. What a shame! Since when do any of us have all that we need? I know I sure don't have enough and maybe at the meeting I will pick up some "nugget of truth" that will be pivotal toward someone's deliverance, or hopefully my own!

Tonda and I have an agreement that we will go anywhere at any time that we feel the water of His love is flowing. We are blessed to have been able to sit under some precious anointed ministries over the last many years. I cannot fathom what treasures that I would have missed out on if I had not gone and listened and had the truth imparted to me from these anointed men and women of God. This book would not have been written if not for the impartation received from these ministries.

I know of a church where the people are frowned upon if they go to meetings where miracles, signs and wonders are likely to happen. That is really backward thinking! I want to be at the meetings where miracles, signs and wonders are taking place because that it the **normal Christian life**. Yes! The normal Christian life is bringing heaven to earth and that means miracles, signs and wonders!

Well, when we were in the receiving barracks, life was becoming more and more uncomfortable. You see we all arrived at Parris Island with our own thoughts, ideas, fantasies and imaginations, but they were going to try and mold us into a strong unit of power where the team was more important than the individual. That is hard work, but they were good at it and a shared hardship was one of the agendas that molded us together. When we first arrived we all would have probably run from the sound of battle, but after 12 weeks of training we were ready to run to the sound of battle.

Over the next 12 weeks the recruits will only get five to six hours of sleep per night, jog and run countless miles, hours and hours of PT (physical training), learn how to march together in unison, swim in full combat gear, rappel from 60-foot towers, practice hand to hand combat, learn bayonet fighting with pugil sticks (looks like a giant Q-tip) run the confidence course, and marksmanship training with both the rifle and .45 cal. handgun. This is all culminated now with an event known as "the Crucible" which lasts almost 60 hours and can only be completed through good teamwork. (See photos on pages 104-109.)

One of the first things that happened to us was the haircut. Today the haircut would be in style, but not in the 60's. We were placed in a barber chair and our head was shaved with electric clippers. I remember one of the guys that had real big "lamb chop" type sideburns—a carry over from Elvis—and the DI asked him if he would like to keep them? "Why yes Sir, I spent a long time growing these. I sure would like to keep them. Can I really keep them?" And the DI replied, "Of course you can—just hold your hands here." At that point he placed each of his hands under each big bushy side burn and said to the recruit, "Catch them!" And catch them he did as the barber shaved them off, and for a couple of weeks he carried them around in his pocket and showed them to the platoon every time the DI told him to. Of course it was not long till they completely dissipated from taking them in and out of his pockets. I still can see the look of astonishment on his face when he caught those sideburns!

Next we were run through a line like a cattle shoot and were dusted with a bug killer (looked like Sevin dust) to kill any mites and lice that had been in our hair or on our bodies.

"782 Gear"

Now the process continued as we were losing our identity and taking on a new identity. We started by taking all of our personal items such as toothbrush, lotions, cream, suntan oil, or other personal effects; packing them up and shipping them back home or throwing them away. The only items you were allowed to keep were a bible and wedding ring. Nothing else! And for safety reasons (it would catch on stuff and tear your finger) you were not allowed to wear the wedding ring, but you had to store it in your foot locker.

The process was really quite simple. They took all of your personal property and gave each of us the exact same thing.

But it was now Marine Corps Green! We all had the same things and no one could be jealous over anything.

Well, what were these things that we all received?

- M-14 rifle
- Bayonet
- Entrenching tool
- Combat boots
- 3 pairs of utility fatigues and web belt
- A cover or 'hat'
- 3 pairs of underwear – tee shirts and boxer shorts
- Shaving supplies
- Toothbrush & Toothpaste
- A shelter half or one half of a two man tent
- A one gallon bucket
- Needles and sewing thread in Marine Corp green
- Duffel bag to carry it all in (still have mine issued to me in September, 1963)

Some interesting stuff to say the least. Why the needle and thread? Simple, the trousers they issued you would fit a giraffe so they had to be shortened to fit each recruit. I was fortunate in that I knew how to sew (well sort of) so I did mine and helped others do theirs. It was a great way to make friends. I also was able to use the thread later to help a fellow recruit sew up an arm wound since he didn't want to go to sick bay for fear he would be set back.[#3]

Okay, how about the bucket? Well, you were able to carry many things in it, you were able to sit on it, you used it to wash your clothes and swab the decks (Marine jargon for mopping the floors).

The process was really quite simple. You let go of all

things that were not pertinent to your life and were given in return the things that were pertinent to your life. At this point, each recruit had exactly the same thing – nothing extra. The recruit was given provision for every need as it came. For instance, we ate three great meals a day that were prepared for us in the mess hall by other Marines pulling that duty. We received dental care if needed, and we each had a dental appointment soon after arriving at the island to check for our needs as some of our guys had never been to a dentist before! Of course we also gave blood samples and were inoculated against who knows what by the corpsman.

Now begins the grueling training which in three short months each recruit learns to march in unison (teamwork), rappel from 60-foot towers, master a obstacle and confidence course, learn hand to hand combat techniques, how to shoot straight and true and how to kill with a bayonet simulated with a pugil stick that looks like a heavy giant Q-tip with boxing gloves on each end. This is all done around extreme physical training by running many miles per day and jogging everywhere you go. Of course we also had constant classes on subjects such as the history of the Marine Corps, the United States Marine Corps Code of Conduct, the USMC Rifle Creed, the USMC rank from private to four star general, the general orders for a sentry, and the Marines Hymn.

Now none of these tasks alone would have been very daunting, but lumped together with the consistent stress and pressure of the DI's constantly all over you it could be emotionally devastating. Some could just not take it. Of course that was part of the plan to see who would fold under the pressure of training—knowing that if they could not take the pressure of training—then they surely could not take the far greater pressure of combat. And combat was what Marines were trained for. And there also was the deeper reason and that was that we would develop strong friendships and start learning that we had to have each other. This was not a one man show or one man training. This was all about the team! What happened was these guys who were basically narcissistic in nature learned through desperation the concept of **Shared Hardships** along with the joy that comes with helping someone other than yourself.

Beloved, this should be the picture of the church as we work together and train together to do battle with our common enemy.

Of course in between these training sessions you were in some kind of class learning things such as the tearing down and cleaning of the M-14 rifle and the .45 caliber pistol. This became such second nature to you that you could do these jobs blindfolded and against a time clock. What seemed impossible at first slowly came together as we did it day after day.

The Marine Corps differs in that it is the only branch of service that every recruit is first and foremost a **skilled marksman**. Let's look at the process the DI's used at Parris Island to achieve this result.

Endnotes: Chapter Three

#1- Cessationist comes from the word cessation and Webster's defines it as "a ceasing, to cease, stop or pause".

Now when this term is applied to theology it means that those folks don't believe in miracles, signs and wonders anymore. They wrongly and falsely believe that miracles, signs and wonders ceased after all the original apostles died. Many will go so far as to say that miracles, signs and wonders are from Satan, but if that is true then Satan is really confused as miracles, signs and wonders were not only used then, but now as well to draw multitudes to Christ. The reason this false theology is so prevalent is because many seminaries and bible schools in America are teaching it.

I understand this problem very well as I grew up in a church that taught cessation, but at the same time taught clearly about Jesus and salvation—really confuses people.

Settle it once and for all—Jesus is still performing healing, deliverances, miracles, signs and wonders and I among many are excited to see Him do these things on a regular basis.

No! He has not changed and if you are not seeing and experiencing these wonderful things, then cry out that God will reveal them to you so you can get with His program!

#2- "Complete not Compete" is discussed in more detail in the 'Honor' Chapter Nine.

#3- To be "set back" meant you would have to join another platoon and not graduate on time—really bad deal! That usually happened if you got sick or hurt and had to go to the sick bay or hospital. If you missed a certain number of training days they would hold or set you back which meant joining another platoon. At that point you would know absolutely no one and your life was miserable, because you had learned to flow with your own platoon and the friendships and bonding were very strong, therefore if you could sew up a wound without going to the hospital you gladly did it!

"THIS IS MY RIFLE"

The creed of the US Marine

"This is my rifle. There are many like it, but this one is mine.

My rifle is my best friend. It is my life. I must master it as I must master my life.

My rifle without me is useless. Without my rifle, I am useless. I must trust my rifle true. I must shoot straighter than my enemy who is trying to kill me. I must shoot him before he shoots me.
I WILL ….

My rifle and I know that what counts in this war in not the rounds we fire, the noise of our burst, nor the smoke we make.
We know that it is the hits that count.
WE WILL HIT….

My rifle is human, even as I, because it is my life. Thus, I will learn it as a brother. I will learn its weaknesses, its strength, its parts, its accessories, its sights and its barrel. I will ever guard it against the ravages of weather and damage as I will ever guard my legs, my arms, my eyes and my heart against damage. I will keep my rifle clean and ready. We will become part of each other.
WE WILL….

Before God, I swear this creed. My rifle and I are the defenders of my country.
We are the masters of our enemy.
WE ARE THE SAVIORS OF MY LIFE….

So be it, until victory is America's and there is no enemy, but only PEACE!"

By: Major General William H. Rupertus (USMC, Ret.)
Written following the attack on Pearl Harbor.

Chapter Four

Some reading this may feel that the rifle creed is a little extreme. Well it is! It has to be! We are in a war and we must not only have good weapons, but we must be trained and able to use them effectively. What good is a weapon if you don't know how to use it? No good at all! It may look good, but it is worthless if you don't know how to use it.

One of the first things we were issued was an M14 rifle, but it was six weeks before we would ever shoot it! Yes six weeks! Why was it so long? Did it sit in a foot locker or the closet or under the bunk? No! Many times No! You lived with it and it truly became a part of you before you ever shot it. We did class after class learning all there was to know about the M14. The M14 had recently replaced the M1 Garand which had been the workhorse rifle for many years. The M1 Garand is still a treasured weapon by many veterans of WWII and Korea. There were 1,380,000 M14 rifles manufactured from 1959 through 1964 and many of them are still in service to-day. The US forces were converted to the M16 about 1966, but the M16 was often referred to as a poodle shooter or a Mattel toy. These disparaging remarks were made because many of the troops in Viet * Nam felt the M16 was frail and underpowered.

Okay, what did we have to learn about it? Well we learned that it weighed 11.5 pounds, was 46.5 inches long with a barrel length of 22 inches and was known as a battle rifle. We learned that it fired a 7.62mm cartridge that was fed by a 20-round detachable box magazine. It would be six long weeks till we fired it and realized that it was capable of accurate fire up to 500 yards. By the way, only in the Marine Corps is each recruit required to qualify at 500 yards. That is the length of 5 football fields and you are required to get the rounds (bullets) in the target. At 500 yards you can barely see the target!

In class after class we took the weapon apart and rebuilt it—time after time we did it until we could do it blindfolded within a minute. Seemed impossible at first, but every recruit learned through the repetitive process—day after day—he would tear it down, and then he would put it back together again. Over and over and over till it became second nature. You could do it without thinking as the rifle had become a part of you!

The DI's knew that there was a good chance that you would end up in the Viet * Nam in horrendous conditions for both man and rifle. The Marine must be able to tear the rifle down, figure out what is wrong with it and put it back together, while lying in a rice paddy at 110 degrees with 90% humidity in total darkness. Oh, did I mention that you were also probably surrounded by enemy troops and your **rifle was your lifeline**? Being able to clean and fix your weapons was not only important to you, but also to your fellow Marines!

What are our weapons?

The apostle Paul made it clear that *"The weapons of our warfare are not carnal but mighty in God for pulling down strongholds"* (2 Corinthians 10:4).

We have now been called to use different weapons, but the training necessary to be an effective warrior is no less strenuous. These weapons must become part of every area of our life so that we use them without even thinking about it! They must become part of our DNA!

First it's the Word!

In the creed of "This is My Rifle" the Marine says: "My rifle is my best friend. It is my life. I must master it as I master my life."

Just as the rifle becomes every Marines best friend and life, so does the **Word of God** become our dear friend and our very life!

Jesus even said talking about himself that *"The Word became flesh and dwelt among us"* (John 1:14a). He is the very Word of God and He desires to dwell among us. Among us means a **very permanent position in a state of rest**. That permanent position in a state of rest is supposed to be in us all the time.

The Marine recruit daily declares that his rifle is his life, but Jesus said, *"Man's life shall be by every word that proceeds from the mouth of God"* (Matthew 4:4). The rifle is a carnal weapon, but the word of God is spiritual—Mighty in God—and it is given that we might pull down the enemy's strongholds of captivity and imprisonment. But we can't use the Word effectively if our training has been slack. We have to be trained to **hit the target** at 500 yards. That's takes time and practice on the firing range.

According to His Word or regarded it not?

There are many dear folks today that due to ignorance of the Word or unbelief in the Word have **regarded it not**. We must be in that company that declares *"Be it unto me according to your word."* If we don't know the Word, then we will not know that still small voice that is speaking to us all the time. We must *"Study and be eager and do your utmost to present yourself to God approved (tested by trial), a workman who has no cause to be ashamed, correctly analyz-*

ing and accurately dividing—rightly handing and skillfully teaching—the Word of Truth" (2 Timothy 2:15 AMP).

Beloved the Word of God is His very **love letter** to us that will instruct us in all the areas of our life, comfort us, reveal His heart and nature, strengthen us and provide the very life of Christ that He wants manifested in the earth. The Word must be our handbook, our guidebook, our battle plans, our marriage manual, our family manual and our life map. The Word must be *"Hidden in our hearts,"* the *"Lamp to our feet,"* and the *"Light to our path," "Our direction to life"* (Psalm 119:11, 105, 116).

Knowing the Word is not just for us, but for the lost, dying and captured world that we have been called to set free.

A Warning Here!

Beloved Warriors, remember that the *"letter kills and the Spirit gives life!"* Let's look at the whole scripture here in 2 Corinthians 3:5-6 to make sure that we get the context of the Apostle Paul's writing and instruction. The Word says: *"Not that we are sufficient of ourselves to think of anything as being from ourselves, but our sufficiency is from God, who made us sufficient as ministers of the new covenant, not of the letter but of the Spirit, for the letter kills, but the Spirit gives life."*

This is critical to comprehend and understand for the Warrior! It is the Spirit that gives life, not the word alone! Does that sound contradictory? It might if you don't understand the difference between the Word and the Spirit.

The Word of God is not just a bunch of letters written on a page that fills a book we call the Bible, but the Word of God is Jesus Himself. Remember that *"In the beginning was the Word, and the Word was with God and the Word was God. He was in the beginning with God. All things were made through Him, and without Him nothing was made that was made. In Him was life, and the life was the light of men"* (John 1:1-4). Jesus is the Word and Jesus is the life. Jesus Himself said *"It is the Spirit who gives life; the flesh profits nothing. The words that I speak to you are spirit, and they are life"* (John 6:63).

You see the *"scriptures that were taught without the power and anointing of God became only the traditions of men creating vain worship for the Pharisees."* The same is true today! Much of what is heard from pulpits is only the tradition of men and causes death, not life. To the Sadducees Jesus said, *"They were mistaken and deceived, not knowing the scriptures nor the power of God."* And to the scribes and Pharisees he said, *"They had elevated their traditions above the commandments of God and therefore they made the Word of God of no effect."* That is still happening today in many circles and it is very subtle and insidious. (Matthew 15:19, 22:29, Mark 7:9 &7:13)

The printed word or the memorized word given out of tradition or legalism is only a 'club' that will often offend the hearer. But a word given with and under the anointing is the *'sword of the Spirit'* and brings impartation and creates life!

Now I trust you understand that I am emphasizing the discipline of learning the Word, but you have to know the **Giver of the word** for the Word to become effective. Learn the Word just as the Marine recruit knew every part of his weapon, but focus on knowing the King of Kings and the Lord of Lords Who makes the word alive!

In order for you to be a Warrior in His kingdom and see signs, wonders and miracles as a normal part of your Christian life you must know what the Word teaches and Who is the teacher!

You must have both the Word and the anointing[#1] in order to be balanced in your walk of love.

As Paul cried out *"That I may know Him and the power of His resurrection,"* (Philippians 3:10) illustrates that our delight and joy will not just be in the mechanics of spiritual discipline; except as those disciplines bring us closer to our Lord and His purposes. Being close and intimate with the King will make you a Warrior who is ready in season and out of season!

Destroy the works of the devil

Beloved Warrior! You have a calling! And it is to set creation free and to destroy the works of the devil. (Romans 8:19, 1 John 3:8b)

We are not fighting in order to win! Jesus has already done that on our behalf at the cross and the resurrection. We are battling now with specific situations where the defeated enemy is still holding ground and constantly testing the Word of God.

For instance, we know that Jesus died in order that all people can be saved. Yet many are not saved because they don't know the truth of the cross or the enemy has blinded their eyes to the provision of God through Jesus. The same thing is true when we look at healing and deliverance. Many are sick, tormented and dis-eased and God wants us to co-labor with Him to set them free! What a calling! What joy to work along side the Creator, the Savior, the Healer and the Deliverer!

Jesus said GO!

Go! (Matthew 28:19) That's not complicated! It is a

direct order from the King of Kings and the Lord of Lords. **Go** is the marching order for the Warriors in this hour. Are all Warriors? No, the Warriors are not **pew warmers**. They are the **Overcomers** that we read about in Hebrews Chapter 11 and Revelation Chapters 2 & 3.

The Warriors are the ones who have been touched by His mighty grace and love and can't help but **Go and Tell** what He has done for them. The Warriors are the ones who know that God is the same yesterday, today and forever and that He still heals, delivers and does awesome signs, wonders and miracles to proclaim His love. The Warriors have heard His voice, experienced His touch and live to co-labor with their Master. They have no greater thrill than to co-labor with their Lord. They are the Sons of Zadok and have come into a deep place of fellowship and intimacy with their God. He is their reason for living and they know the truth that they are Eternal and that they are a part of Him. They know that they are set apart for His use and to love Him with all their heart, with all their soul, with their entire mind, and with all their strength and love their neighbor as themselves.

They are totally free to live, as they know that death has been swallowed up in victory!

They will **Go** anywhere and face any foe knowing that *"To be absent from the body is be present with the Lord."*

They know that just like Timothy they are to *"Preach the word! Be ready in season and out of season. Convince, rebuke, exhort with all longsuffering and teaching"* (2 Timothy 4:2).

But to be effective you must be diligent in your training and discipline of the Word!

How does a Warrior train?

He or she trains like their life depends on the training! Because it does! There are no short cuts to a Warrior's training and without a desire to stand in the gap and find your place on the wall[#2] you will never be ready for the battle.

Okay, let's look at some principles that have worked for many warriors throughout history.

"I Will" won't cut it!

Self Determination may be our biggest enemy! Self determination will always lead to trouble and it disguises itself skillfully. Self determination actually brings us under a curse for in Jeremiah 17:5-6 the Lord says: *"Cursed is the man who trusts in man and makes flesh his strength. Whose heart departs from the Lord. For he shall be like a shrub in the desert, and shall not see when good comes. But he shall inhabit the parched places in the wilderness, in a land which is not inhabited."* This is a tough issue because we are taught and trained to be self-sufficient. That is fine so long as you are under the direction of the Lord as you do it. The pride of America is to be a self-made man and literally my whole life in the education system was geared to what I could do for me! All the while missing the calling that "you are not your own, you belong to another as you have been bought with a high price and "that the greatest among you shall be your servant."

My experience in ministering to folks who are tormented in body and soul is that most are **Self Determined**. Self Determination leads to ginormous issues of pride and we know that "pride comes before the fall" and of course rebellion is walking right with the pride. The classic example of self-determination, pride and rebellion is found in the fall of

Lucifer in Isaiah the 14th chapter. *"How you are fallen from heaven, O Lucifer, son of the morning! How you are cut down to the ground, you weakened the nations! For you have said in your heart;*

I will ascend into heaven.

I will exalt my throne above the stars of God;

I will also sit on the mount of the congregation on the farthest sides of the north;

I will ascend above the heights of the clouds,

I will be like the Most High.

Yet you shall be brought down to Sheol, to the lowest depths of the pit.

Those who see you will gaze at you and consider you, saying: Is this the man who made the earth tremble, who shook kingdoms, who made the world as a wilderness, and destroyed its cities, who did not open the house of his prisoners"

(Isaiah 14:12-17 NKJ)

The damning words here are **"I will!"** Those two words were the reflection of his heart for it is true that "out of the abundance of the heart the mouth speaks." Because of the trickery in the garden and the decision to listen to the **"I will"** voice we too are now born with the nature to live in the **"I will"** realm! But praise God we have been redeemed through the Lord Jesus fulfilling the Father's plan. And now we can make the choice to say: ***"Not my will, but your will Lord!"*** Those are liberating words indeed. Scary at first, but very liberating!

The true life of the Warrior is only found in **Surrender!**

66

Don't panic! There is an answer!

Okay, don't get discouraged! There is an answer! The answer is in Jeremiah 17:7-8:

"Blessed is the man who trusts in the Lord, and whose
hope is in the Lord. Amen
For he shall be like a tree planted by the waters, which
spread out its roots by the river.
And will not fear when heat comes:
but its leaf will be green.
And will not be anxious in the year of drought, nor will
cease from yielding fruit."

Now those are encouraging words indeed! Do you believe them? The choice is ours: **Do we want to trust in man, including yourself, and be a shrub in the desert and inhabit the parched places in the wilderness, or do we want to trust in the Lord and be a tree planted by the waters—that will not fear the heat—will not be anxious—and never cease from bearing fruit!** Wow! The difference is in the choice!

The issue here is really the will of God. What does God say about any given situation? Are we listening to His voice or are we running after every other solution? You are not your own, you belong to Him! That should change everything —the way you think—the way you act—the very core of your life!

A Warrior's Resolve!

I remember the words of the officer in the movie *"The Dirty Dozen."* They were classic! When the Colonel inspected the "Dozen" that were being volunteered to go on a deadly mission he said to the training Sgt. **"They look good, but**

can they fight?" In other words do they have Resolve? [#3] **Resolve** is defined as **"Unwavering firmness of character or action, and fixed purpose or intention."**

That is a good responsible question and one that the DI's tried to determine when we were at Parris Island. Who had resolve and who didn't? They wanted to know now while we were in training because the **battle field** was no place to make that determination.

Being super strong in body, a great athlete, an inspiring intellectual does not make the Warrior! Now, none of those things were harmful, in fact they were helpful. But the main issue was the **Heart**! Did he or she have the heart to fight? Are they willing to take the battle to the enemy at any cost? Can they lay down their life for their brothers and the cause? In other words, do you have the **"Resolve" (unwavering firmness of character or action, and fixed purpose or intention)** to carry through the mission; only looking for the prize in the high calling of our King Christ Jesus.

You see a Warrior knows that Colossians 3:1-3 is very true for him: *"If then you be raised with Christ, seek those things which are above, where Christ is, sitting at the right hand of God. Set your mind (affection) on things above, not on things on the earth. For you died and your life is hidden with Christ in God."* A Warrior is willing to fight for the call that God has entrusted Him with and the warrior is willing to leave the results in God's hands! A true Warrior knows that he is already dead... dead in Christ... But his life is hidden with Christ in God, and that means **life evermore.**

Endnotes: Chapter Four

#1- We must be careful not just to know about Him in the sense of book knowledge, but to know Him intimately... to hear His voice... to know His grace and love... to know His will and desire to heal and restore... to know His power to move in signs, wonders and miracles. I have actually talked with educated men steeped in the study of the scriptures, but they did not know HIM!

Our heart's cry must be as Paul's... "That I may know Him and the power of His resurrection"

#2- In late December of 2007 the Lord spoke a clear prophetic word to me concerning 'Standing on the Wall'! This word has been confirmed over and over, through apostolic ministry as well as many others in the body of Christ.

Here is the word!

"These truths are not only for you and your family, but also for all that you come in contact with through the ministry as well as everyday life. Proclaim this word: That this is the appointed time—the Kairos moment—and this is the time to climb the wall* and stand in your place!" "Don't be concerned where your place on the wall is for I will show you your place if you ask me and seek me according to Matthew 6:33, *"Seek first the Kingdom of God and His righteousness and all these things will be added to you."*

My heart (Father's heart) is that your joy be fulfilled as you stand with one hand holding a construction tool and the other hand holding a weapon. Many have been discouraged, discomforted, frustrated, ready even to give up, despairing, sometimes even of life, but I the Lord of Hosts have made a way for the battle to be fought that the victory that I have won will also be yours experientially... But the primary focus is to be on others first... Not yourself. This is the hour of GIVING... All are being called to give some, and some will be called to give all! His nature and His joy are in giving, and as you give on the wall... your life and your family's life will flourish as never before.

This is not a spectator event ... this is War! Now is not the time to sit, but the time to Stand & Fight**... Stand and see His salvation... cooperate with Him... work with Him... follow the Captain of your salvation... praise, worship and adore Him... and His glory will be like a river that never runs dry and the force of which is cleansing and refreshing. As you stand in the battle your eyes will be opened to see the heavenly host that has been sent for YOU. They will strengthen you, comfort you as you stand! I long to visit you and take you deeper into my glorious river. Yes! Even as you stand in the midst of the battle there will be a river flowing from your very belly... the River of Life of which there is no end! The river that I have sent for the healing of the nations and the restoration of all things!

*Ezekiel 22:30 *"So I sought for a man among them who would make a wall, and stand in the gap before Me on behalf of the land, that I would not destroy it: **but I found no one.**"*

Nehemiah 4:14 *"When I saw their fear, I rose and spoke to the nobles, the officials and the rest of the people: Do not be afraid of them; remember the Lord who is great and awesome, and **fight for your brothers, your sons, your daughters, your wives and your houses."*

#3- Resolve is not only important in warfare, but also in spiritual warfare! The most unfortunate thing that happened in Viet Nam was when the US pulled out and left the people with no support or protection. Credible evidence reveals that our lack of Resolve preempted the death of close to two million Cambodians. The military had the Resolve to win the war, but the politicians and the public under the influence of the press lacked the back bone or resolve to finish the job! The very forces of evil that we had vowed to fight and destroy won the "media mind game" and caused us to flee leaving the Vietnamese and Cambodian people helpless against a stronger invading force. Lack of Resolve caused us to flee!

"You Ain't Gonna Like Losing"

President Bush did make a bad mistake in the war on terror. But the mistake was not his decision to go to war in Iraq.

Bush's mistake came in the belief that this country is the same one that his father fought for in WWII. It is not!

Back then, they had just come out of a vicious depression. The country was steeled by the hardship of that depression, but they had believed fervently in this country. They knew that the people had elected leaders, so it was the people's duty to back those leaders.

Therefore when the war broke out the people came together, rallied behind, and stuck with their leaders, whether they had voted for them or not,
or whether the war was going badly or not.

And war was just as distasteful and the anguish just as great then as it is today. Often there were more casualties in one day in WWII than we have had in the entire Iraq war. But that did not matter. The people stuck with the President because it was their patriotic duty. Americans put aside their differences in WWII and worked together to win that war.

Everyone from every strata of society, from young to old pitched in. Small children pulled little wagons around to gather scrap metal for the war effort. Grade school students saved their pennies to buy stamps for war bonds to help the effort.

Men who were too old or medically 4F lied about their age or condition trying their best to join the military. Women doubled their work to keep things going at home. Harsh rationing of everything from gasoline to soap, to butter was imposed, yet there was very little complaining.

You never heard prominent people complaining on the radio belittling the President. Interestingly enough in those days there were no 'fat cat actors and entertainers' who ran off to visit and fawn over dictators of hostile countries and complain to them about our President. Instead, they made upbeat films and entertained our troops to help the troops' morale. And a bunch of them even enlisted.

And imagine this: Teachers in schools actually started the day off with a Pledge of Allegiance and with prayers for our country and troops!

Back then, no newspaper would have dared point out certain weak spots in our cities where bombs could be set off to cause the maximum damage. No newspaper would dared have complained about what we were doing to catch spies.

A newspaper would have been laughed out of existence if it had complained that the German or Japanese prisoners were being 'tortured' by being forced to wear women's underwear, or subjected to interrogation by a woman, or being scared by a dog or did not have air conditioning.

There were a lot of things different back then. We were not subjected to a constant barrage of pornography, perversion and promiscuity in movies or on radio. We did not have legions of crack-heads, dope pushers and armed gangs roaming our streets.

No, President Bush did not make a mistake in his handling of the war on terrorism. He made the mistake of believing that we still had the courage and fortitude of our fathers. He believed that this was still the country that our fathers fought so dearly to preserve.

It is not the same country. It is now a cross between Sodom and Gomorrah and the "Land of Oz". We did unite for a short while after 9/11, but our attitude changed when we found out that defending our country would require some sacrifices.

We are in great danger! The terrorists are fanatic Muslims. They believe that it is okay, even their duty, to kill anyone who will not convert to Islam. It has been estimated that about one third or over three hundred million Muslims are sympathetic to the terrorists cause. Hitler and Tojo combined did not have nearly that many potential recruits.

So... we either win it—or lose it—and
"You Ain't Gonna Like Losing!"

America and the church are not at war. The military is at war. America and the church are at the mall!!

'Author Unknown'

Many of you reading "You Ain't Gonna like Losing" feel that it is extreme. It is not! I for one have seen the dramatic attitudes of our citizens' change over the last 50 years, and I don't think it is extreme at all. I trust you understand that I am more concerned about the principalities and powers that are behind the evil forces of radical, fanatical Muslims than the fanatical Muslims themselves (fanatical Muslims are only one tool the enemy is using in this hour). They are driven by the wicked one and his desire to kill any and everything that is Christian. They are his current puppets and he is using them to try and achieve that objective!

Make no mistake! In the natural we are definitely in grave danger in the USA of losing to fanatic forces, but our main concern is how the enemy (Luciferian spirit) is at work behind the scenes.

As a minister I am gravely concerned that the church, for the most part, does not even have a grasp of the spiritual danger we are in. The complacency and lack of discernment regarding our natural and spiritual condition in America, especially in the church, is both horrifying and appalling. We are imploding on ourselves because most Christians don't even believe that there is a spiritual war!

Let's look at some areas where we are losing and I don't like it!

Chapter Five

What Are We Fighting For?

So I stationed armed guards at the most vulnerable
places of the wall and assigned people by families with
their swords, lances, and bows. After looking things
over I stood up and spoke to the nobles, officials, and
everyone else: "Don't be afraid of them. Put your minds
on the Master, great and awesome, and then fight for
your brothers, your sons, and your daughters, your
wives, and your homes."

(Nehemiah 4:13-14 MSG)

Were these men standing on the wall warriors? Was Nehemiah a gallant fighting man? No! Not that we have any record of. He had been the cup-bearer to King Artaxerxes which was a position of deep trust and devotion! He came to Jerusalem with a heart and word to rebuild the wall and restore Jerusalem as a fortified city. The Jews had been thwarted on every side with extreme threats and bluff of force; as well as manipulation and intrigue to get orders from the Persian court to stop the work. It was a very desperate situation!

History has often proven that average men will respond in desperate times. That is what happened to America during WWII. Ordinary men and women responded to the call 'to stand on the wall' and defend the cause of freedom and liberty. They had a 'Resolve' that said we are going to fight for our brothers, our sons, our daughters, our wives and our homes! They said we are not going to stand by and be run over either from the west or from the east. The cost was horrific in terms of loss of life, but men like my father serving in the Pacific theatre knew that the cost was worth it to preserve our freedom!

'Fight for your Brothers'
"You Ain't Gonna Like Losing"

"By this we know love, because He laid down His life for us. And we also ought to lay down our lives for the brethren" (1 John 3:16).

There is a bonding between warriors that is hard to find in any other arena of life. This is the deep bonding of brothers—training for and fighting for a 'cause' higher than themselves and considering each other worthy of double honor. A bond that is so strong these warriors will gladly lay down their own life for their brother.

What higher calling and purpose is there than helping our Savior Brother establish His kingdom of life and righteousness in the earth? Wow! Does your heart cry "sign me up"? Probably if you are reading this book you have already signed up and know that our Lord is not asking for applications, but commitments!

Many have signed up for the work of the ministry only to find that the trials, despair, tribulations, disappointments, heartbreaks and betrayals were not what they expected! I can't tell you how many Pastors, Missionaries, and other devoted servants of the Lord that have shared with me their despair with the ministry. I have had these opportunities as the ministry God has opened up for us has been one of 'Restoring' the broken and defeated in the battle.

I too have personally experienced these defeats and discouragements; and at times been ready to 'head to the hills' leaving all of this ministry stuff behind. Fortunately at those times my Father reminds me that I signed up for the 'long haul' and He will let me know when the journey is over. No quitting until then!

Just how bad is the problem with frustration and

discouragement in the ministry? The following well known facts reflect the despair:[#1]

- 80% of ministers leave the ministry within the first five years
- 70% have no close friend, confidant or mentor
- 70% are in depression
- 80% of pastors and 84% of their spouses are discouraged or in despair
- 80% of minister's adult children end up in depression

For me one of the words that God gave me to hold on to was Hebrews 6:12: *"That you do not become sluggish, but imitate those who through faith and patience inherit the promises."* Who are some of these that we can imitate? Well, there is Abraham, Moses, Joshua, Elijah, Samuel, Elisha, Paul and the apostles; and of course Jesus the author of our salvation walked it out as a Warrior on the earth.

You may feel that you are not trained or ready for the battle. Well, you probably aren't! But that is not even the issue at this point. Again the issue is a matter of resolve! Are your Savior Brother and your spiritual brothers worth fighting for and even giving your life for? Yes they are!

Remember when Jesus said to Peter *"Will you lay down your life for my sake?"* And because Peter did not have 'the fight' in him yet he had brazenly responded that *"He would lay his life down for the Lord's sake."* But those words haunted him later as he heard the rooster crow those three awful times. What tragedy! What despair! What hopelessness!

In a moment, the tragedy, the despair and the hopelessness were all swallowed up as the Lord Jesus spoke the 'rhema' word to Peter. *"Peter do you love me... then feed my sheep."* He spoke it to him three times, well establishing His deep love and covenant with Peter. Wow! At that moment 'Resolve' was established in Peter's heart once again, he had '**his**

fight' back. He knew that he was ready and willing to follow the master even unto death. Peter never looked back and did indeed years later give his life for his beloved king choosing to be crucified upside down.

Now Peter was a Spiritual Warrior! He was trained and would go forward from that moment to be a 'rock' and a mighty force to help establish the Kingdom... the true Kingdom... which is the kingdom of our Lord and His Christ! This is the kingdom we are being trained for, and the kingdom that is truly worth fighting for. This is an eternal kingdom which will never end!

We are fighting to see the establishment of these words: *"The kingdoms of this world have become the kingdoms of our Lord and of His Christ, and He shall reign forever and ever"* (Revelation 11:15).

'Fight for Your Sons & Daughters'
"You Ain't Gonna Like Losing"

There is no doubt that our enemy is determined to destroy our children and the wicked one never tires of his quest for their destruction!

We read in Exodus where the King of Egypt said unto the midwives who were helping birth the Hebrew children: *"When you do the duties of the midwife for the Hebrew women, and see them on the birth stools, if it is son, then you shall kill him, but if it is a daughter, then she shall live"* (Exodus 1:16). And again we see in verse 22: *"Pharaoh commanded all his people saying, 'Every son who is born you shall cast into the river, and every daughter you shall save alive."*

Now some thousands of years later the enemy makes a big play to wipe out the coming of the 'Anointed One' knowing that He is the deliverer. Matthew 2:16 records that *"Herod, when he saw that he was deceived by the wise men, was exceedingly angry; and he sent forth and put to death all the male children who were in Bethlehem and in all its districts, from two years old and under."*

Beloved, we are in a spiritual war and the church is in many ways totally unaware; and certainly not trained or prepared to meet and defeat the enemy. Reality is that the enemy is determined to *"kill, steal and destroy"* the anointing wherever he sees it manifested.

Statistics show that 'born again Christian' students will lose their faith within the first 30 days of attending college or university. Most of these students have never been taught what to expect and they are therefore overwhelmed with the onslaught of demonic teaching that usually begins with the declaration that the bible is not the word of God. This was the serpent's tactic with Eve in the garden to question whether God was believable or not. The serpent succeeded with Eve and his strategy has not changed! The enemy knows when he has a winning hand and he keeps playing it over and over. His tactics are often very predictable!

Our sons and daughters are worth fighting for! And who is going to fight for them if we don't? Are you standing on the wall for them in fasting and prayer?

'Abuse of our sons and daughters'
"You Ain't Gonna Like Losing"

A horrible sad tragedy is occurring daily in our homes across America. Untold children are suffering at the hands of their fathers and mothers, as well as other people who have responsibility over them. The numbers are staggering!

There is a hidden epidemic of child abuse in the US that is shameful! There are over 3,000,000 reported cases of abuse each year! Yes! 3,000,000 reported cases of abuse and authorities estimate that this number is only a third of the true cases. If that is true, then there are over 9,000,000 children abused in their own homes in the US each year.[#2]

We know for a fact that at least 4.1 kids die every day in their own home! Yes! That is 4.1 per day die at the hands of the ones that are supposed to be loving them and nurturing them! 4.1 deaths per day equal almost 1,500 kids who die every year in American homes. Now consider that since the war in Iraq has started that 4,000 of our troops have died. That is a time period of over five years, yet during that same five plus years we have killed over 8,000 of our own children! Is it possible that our own American homes are as dangerous as the battlefield? Okay, I know that comparison is a stretch, but we need to get hold of some reality here and realize— what are we fighting for!

Where are the people protesting the killing of our own children? Come on let's be honest with ourselves. This is not theory. This is hard reality! 8,000 children have died in American homes as hopeless victims; while 4,000 brave men and women have died serving their country in an honorable fashion. Now my desire would have been that no one died during this time—at war or in the home—but truth is truth, and it is obvious that we have our concentration in the wrong place when it comes to protests! Our priorities are really messed up!

Another frightening fact is that three women are murdered every day by their husband or boyfriend! Yes, every day three of our daughters, sisters and wives are being murdered!

Come on church! Where are you? Are you really at the mall while your own children are suffering in your own home? Where is the outrage? Where is the clamor for action?

Where is the demand for our political leaders to move on behalf of our children? We should all be angry and up in arms at the outrageous injustice that is occurring in our homes as a silent epidemic of abuse is raging in our nation, the land of the free and the home of the brave!

Okay church, are you willing to stand on the wall and be counted as a *"warrior"* for the innocent ones that cannot protect themselves? Are you willing to find a place in the gap of horror and *"fight"* for righteousness and justice?

'Sexual Abuse'
"You Ain't Gonna like Losing"

Can it get worse? We would hope not, but again we have to be honest and deal with the tragic facts that are indisputable. Those facts determine that it is getting worse, not better!

The issues of sexual abuses are staggering and frankly I would consider the data suspect if I had not personally dealt with so many people who have been victimized. And remember that most of the people I deal with, or pray with are folks in the church. As a street cop and police chaplain I saw the sexual abuse first hand, but it did not become real to me until I saw how prevalent it was in the church. On this issue, as well as most issues, there is little difference between the church and the unchurched. Sad, but true!

I remember one of my first ministry sessions with a young woman who was having a difficult time with her marriage because of 'trust and betrayal' issues. I could discern that she had issues with men in general and her father had not helped in the least, always accusing her of promiscuity and other word curses during her adolescence. She soon began to trust me and confided that her fear and trust issues with men had started in the church when she was 14-years-old.

"Pastor Ish," she said, "It happened on a camping trip with the youth group when one of the deacons who had gone to chaperone us forced himself on me sexually. I had gone down to the lake by myself, and suddenly he was there making all kinds of suggestive comments about how good I looked in my bathing suit. I was sort of flattered that he would even notice as my dad had never said anything nice about me. Later that night he snuck into my tent and asked me to meet him at the lake side. I went thinking it would be exciting and that other kids would be there. But there were no other kids there and he raped me right there on the beach!"

As I was about to pray with her over this old traumatic wound and the defilement that comes with it she said: "Oh there's more. I finally got up the courage to tell my Dad about it and he said that I was making it all up just to get attention. Then a week later when I got more courage and at the encouragement of some friends I made an appointment to see the pastor. I shared with the pastor what had happened and he replied 'that I probably had made a sexual move on the deacon'! And then the pastor raped me behind the locked door! That was my introduction to church! After that I could not trust any men!"

It was another 15 years before that gal stepped a foot into church. The good news is that God touched her and healed her of all that horrible junk as she came to a place of releasing and forgiving these men for their sins against her.[#3]

Known statistics show that one out of every four girls will be sexually abused by the time she is 18, and one out of every six boys will have suffered some kind of sexual abuse also by the age of 18;[#4] and consider the frightening part is that stat is only of the abuses reported. The story I just told about the girl being raped on the camping trip was never reported. As are countless others never reported!

Unfortunately I have ministered to many women and

men who have suffered similar abuse.

'Abortion'
"You Ain't Gonna like losing"

How has such a simple issue become so complicated? The issue is simple because a human life starts at the moment of conception! But it gets complicated because the 'wicked one' has promoted an agenda that enhances and promotes 'choice' over 'common sense' and solid—yes, rock solid—medical evidence that supports that life begins at conception!

It gets complicated because the scripture is clear in 2 Corinthians 3:14: *"That their minds were blinded."* This does not mean that they were literally blinded, but it was like a cloud of smoke was over their heads and they could not see. Could not see what? They could not see the truth even though it was right before them. It is truly a deep deception. And of course when you are deceived you don't know it because you are deceived! Deception is one of the major weapons that the wicked one uses and he uses it very effectively.

What is the antidote to the poison of deception? The antidote is 'Truth'! The truth makes you free and nothing else will set you free (John 8:36).

Okay, how bad is the deception on abortion? Let's look at some undeniable statistics.[5]

- There are approximately 1.4 million abortions annually in the United States.
- There are approximately 3,700 abortions 'every day' in the United States.
- Black women are 4 times more likely to have an abortion.

- Protestant women have 37% of all abortions.

- Catholic women account for 31% of all abortions.

- Jewish women account for 1.3% of all abortions.

- Women with no religious affiliation account for 24% of abortion.

- 18% of all abortions in America are performed on women who identify themselves as being 'born again' Christians.

Do you find it alarming that at least one of six women who have an abortion claims to be a born again follower of Jesus Christ? At this point in my life I do find it appalling, but there was a time as a Christian that I did not have a clue that life begins at conception. And I saw 'abortion' as a convenient way to correct a problem—that of some pregnant gal—that was not married. I was one of those that were blinded by the wicked one and my own desires. I did not want to face the truth.

Here is my story! I got a gal pregnant when I was in my 20's while on leave in the Marine Corps. She called me and let me know that she was pregnant (we lived in different towns) and after some discussion we decided that the best thing to do was to get an abortion. She knew a Doctor who would do it and I helped fund the procedure. At the time, it seemed like no big deal. But it was a big deal! I found myself seeing little babies all over the place and thinking "Could that have been my child?"

As I got older the thoughts in my mind did not go away —they only grew stronger. I would do the math in my head and see kids who would be the same age as my aborted child and I would agonize over the decision to abort! What started out as no big deal was getting bigger and bigger all the time. It became a torment to me. And the guilt and shame was sometimes overwhelming. People have trouble admitting it, but they instinctively know that they have taken a life through abortion. There needs to be healing and deliverance from the torment and guilt.

It was many years later that 'by the grace of God' I was freed from that torment of guilt and shame. You see there is 'no sin' that can't be forgiven, but we have to agree with God on the issue and confess and repent (1 John 1:7).

Now years later I have the joy of helping other folks who have had abortions—either male or female—find the freedom from the torment of abortion.[#6]

Ministering Redemptive Love

I long to see the church take the place of 'Ministering Redemptive Love' to the countless thousands that have experienced abortions! We have unwittingly been more agents of judgment, than vessels of love!

We must as ministers of reconciliation remember that *"Mercy triumphs over judgment"* and that we are called to *"Bear one another's burdens, and restore in the spirit of gentleness remembering that we too are tempted and capable of falling flat when we think we are so strong."* (James 2:13, Galatians 6:1-3, 1 Corinthians 10:12)

Self righteousness and spiritual pride have no place in this war for the unborn! If you look at Galatians 5:19-21 at the works of the flesh—sin—you will see that murder (abortion) is tucked right in between envy and drunkenness! Oh, and lets not forget the serious sin issues of bitterness and unforgiveness! They are killers—just a different type!

We talk about how wrong and immoral abortion is—and it is—but are we willing as followers of Jesus to make a path of love for these pregnant girls? What kind of path am I talking about? Are we willing to take these pregnant, devastated unmarried girls into our churches or our homes and care for their needs, materially, financially and spiritually? We must get this love ministry to where 'Saints' are standing on the wall with them to retake the lost ground that the enemy has stolen – without bringing further condemnation and shame on them. Remember these sons and daughters are dearly loved by our Father and they have a great destiny in His kingdom.

Will we stand on the wall as **'Watchmen'** to help restore their dignity, their value and their eternal calling in Christ Jesus?

I believe the words of Isaiah are applicable here as we stand on the wall for our brothers, our sons and daughters, our wives and our homes.

*On your walls, O Jerusalem, I have appointed **watchmen**; All day and night they will never keep silent. You, who remind the Lord, take no rest for yourselves!*

Isaiah 62:6 NASB

Endnotes: Chapter Five

#1- Information taken from an article "Happy Shiny Pastors" found on www.blogchristainitytoday.com quoting sources "Focus on the Family and Barna Research Group.

#2- www.childhelp.org, Prevent child abuse North Carolina a non-profit organization.

#3-You can read more about the effects of someone else's sin on you in my book "Life in the Red Zone". The teaching is on page 92. Books are available at: www.restoringhearts.net.

#4- www.theresnoexcuse.com.

#5- Thanks to Tara Quinn, founder & Director of H.E.L.P. for her assistance in this research. She and her team are true 'Warriors' standing in the gap for the unborn. You can contact her at: www.monroehelpcpc.org.

#6- Linda Lange is a wonderful minister to help folks through the pain and agony of abortion. You can contact her on her website at: www.lifeapplicationministries.org.

Deanne Day is a team member of Restoring Hearts who has much success in bringing people through the trauma of sexual abuse as well as abortion. You can contact her at: www.Restoringhearts.net

Joseph spoke these words!

"But as for you, you meant evil against me; but God meant it for good, in order to bring it about as it is today, to save many people alive"

Genesis 50:20

Only a Righteous man with his character trained by the Spirit of God as a Warrior and knowing the faithfulness of his God could make such a statement!

Chapter Six

Warrior's Walk = Joseph

Who are some of the most notable warriors in the Bible? My first thought is always Joshua and Caleb as they stood strong for 40 years waiting on the Israelites to get their act together and take the "Promised Land." They knew how to fight and they were warriors from the get go. Then there is also King David! Wow! What a warrior!

These were hardened men who had extensive *battle training* and would fight anything from a lion, bear, giants, Canaanites, Moabites, Amorites and all sort of other evil 'ites'. These men were not afraid of the battle, but would actually run to the battle! Most of the time there was no fear with these warriors. They had the fight in them and were always ready for the battle.

They remind me of some of the *'ole salty Marines* [1] I was deployed on board ship with. When they thought we were getting ready for battle they sat and sharpened their K-Bar combat knife until it was like a surgical tool. These men were hardened veterans—many from the Korean War and a few from WWII. Civilians thought some of these guys were scary, but for us young guys they were a comfort. They had been there and come back. And were now willing to go again, battle scars and all! That is the heart of a warrior—there is a job to do and I have been called to do it, so let's get it on!

Am I scared? You bet I am! But the words of the Lord to Joshua ring true in our spirit: *"Be strong and of good courage; do not be afraid, nor be dismayed, for the Lord your God is with you wherever you go"* (Joshua 1:9).

Saints! We have a battle that God has called us to and He has given us the same word He gave to Joshua. *"Be strong and of good courage; do not be afraid, nor be dismayed, for the Lord your God is with you wherever you go."* Yes, wherever you go! Whether that is into the lion's den, the battle for your family and country, or maybe like the prison that Joseph was put into! God is there with us and will strengthen us in the midst of the battle!

"The Warrior's Walk" of Joseph

Beloved, we are so blessed to be living in this hour! Our heavenly Father is pouring out His word and His revelation truth in a measure that has never been experienced before. What a joy for those who have *"eyes to see and ears to hear,"* but the real joy is for those who are willing to walk in obedience to that word which they have heard the Father say!

Learning the truth, knowing the truth, and even expounding the truth, is not, nor will it ever be the same as **Walking** in the truth. Unfortunately, the church in this hour has a lot of learners, but only a few walkers.

Is there a key or a truth that we need to get hold of in order to become a walker and not just a learner? In 2 Peter 1:3-4, we are told: *"His divine power has given to us all things that pertain to life and godliness, through the knowledge of Him who called us by glory and virtue, by which have been given to us exceedingly great and precious promises, that through these you may be partakers of the divine nature, having escaped the corruption that is in the world through lust."*

Now it says very clearly that we have already been given everything we need to be partakers of His divine nature—so what are we lacking? I believe that part of what we are lacking is some basics to walk as a "Warrior."

Why Basics?

If you are looking for some deep, esoteric revelation from the third heaven, then this writing is probably not for you. On the other hand, if you find yourself discouraged, or in the midst of a fiery trial and wondering what God is doing in your life, then I believe that this is for your encouragement and edification. If you realize that you have had an initial experience (born again) with God, been baptized in the Holy Spirit, but know in your heart that you are not where you should be, then this teaching may well be for you!

Joseph - a Special Restorer!

I want to look at Joseph's life. He was a man used mightily by God, but he went through fiery trials and testing before he was able to be manifested as God's instrument of grace and deliverance. I believe that this pattern is repeated many times in scripture with various people, but I want to look primarily at Joseph's life. His life is so important because it reveals the current condition of many Saints that have *"eyes to see and ears to hear."* If you will look closely at Joseph's life I believe you will find that your spiritual life will be closely paralleled—if you are being diligent to move in your calling.

Joseph was the son of Jacob, the grandson of Issac and the great grandson of Abraham. We could look at many warriors in the bible, but I want to look at Joseph as there is no record that he was ever trained as a "Warrior." But for me he exemplifies ***"The Warrior's Walk,"*** as he lived to please his God regardless of the circumstances! And many of his circumstances were pure 'hell'—make no mistake about it! He was a victim many times, but did not take on the victim mentality. Why? He knew who he was even in the midst of the fire and knew that God was on his side and working for and through him!

Okay, let's look at some simple principles that separated Joseph unto the ministry that God had called him for.

Righteousness

The first one is "**Righteousness!**"

What made Joseph different from his older brothers? Certainly training had to have played a part in forming his mind toward God. Somewhere and somehow before the age of 17 Joseph had learned to have a deep trust in the God of his fathers. This trust would later carry Joseph through some horrendous times, which we will look at in some detail later on.

Joseph was the 11th son of Jacob, but the first born of Jacob's second wife Rachel – who Jacob loved more than his first wife Leah. There was much contention in this blended family, not only between Rachel and Leah, but also between Jacob and Labon. Labon was Joseph's grandfather on his mother's side. Jacob had been very busy trying to get what he wanted and all this time there was a very real fear lingering in his mind about his brother Esau; who had vowed to kill Jacob for his deceitful act of stealing the blessing from their father Issac.[#2]

We also know that although Jacob had a relationship with his God; that he was slack concerning the training of his family. Obviously, Rachel was still clinging to the gods of her father, or she would not have stolen them when they departed his country. Did Rachel unwittingly put a curse on herself and her family when she stole the idols and then lied about it? I think she did![#3] Given the fact that all ten brothers had some part in selling their brother Joseph would be more than enough proof that they were lacking in proper moral and spiritual development—not to mention some of the other sins the brothers were involved in!

It seems that following the slaughter of Hamor and Shechem and the massacre of all the men along with the looting and taking captive the women and children, that Jacob realized his family was out of control. He saw that their spiritual base was the problem. Granted the brothers had cause to be indignant following the seducing and defilement of their only sister Dinah, but they went way too far in dealing with Hamor and Shechem.

Even when Jacob rebuked them for their horrible actions they were defensive and still trying to justify themselves![#4] They were doing then what we still like to do today—and that is finding someone or something else to blame in order to justify our wrong actions and attitudes!

Family Meeting!

God spoke to Jacob and told him to go to Bethel! Now that God had Jacob's attention again, he called a family meeting! He not only called his own family, but also all those that were gathered in their midst. The scripture does not say it, but I can hear him saying *"Okay! Enough is enough; let's get back to some basics."*

However the scripture does say that Jacob said to his household: *"Put away the foreign gods that are among you, purify yourselves, and change your garments. Then let us arise and go up to Bethel; and I will make an altar there to God, who answered me in the day of my distress and has been with me in the way which I have gone. So they gave Jacob all the foreign gods which were in their hands and the earrings which were in their ears; and Jacob hid them under the terebinth tree which was by Shechem"* (Genesis 35:2-4).

You might wonder why Jacob waited all these years to try and establish spiritual things in his family. It seems kind of late now that the kids were older and well established in bad and harmful patterns. It seems that Jacob was like so many fathers, busy about making more and more money and trying to figure out how to beat the system. He was now reaping what he had planted and he did not like it[#5]. It seems that he knew he was going to have to change his ways with his young son Joseph. In his heart he knew the truth: *"Train up a child in the way he should go, and when he is old he will not depart from it"* (Proverbs 22:6).

Prior to this time Jacob had wrestled with God and held on until he blessed him! Jacob had been told at that time that he would no longer be called Jacob but Israel—that he had held on and prevailed and would have power with God and with man![#6]

Church, can we hold on and prevail in order to manifest His glory! That is our calling and that is what the war is about. It will take the **"The Warrior's Walk"** to walk in that glory!

The lad Joseph benefited from his father's experiences. Jacob now realized that he had made serious mistakes with his older children and he determined to command in ways that he did not do with the older ones. No doubt, Jacob was diligent in training and instructing Joseph in the ways of their Father God. Many precious times were had with father and son sitting and discussing the holiness and obedience that God was looking for in people. I believe that Jacob was now humble enough to even share the mistakes he had made. No doubt he shared with Joseph the ways God had broken and molded him to the point of a name change—which represents a change in 'nature'.

Grandfather Isaac's influence

Although the scripture does not say anything about the relationship between Joseph and his grandfather Isaac, it is certainly likely that Isaac had a tremendous influence in Joseph's training. Isaac was still alive when Jacob went into Bethel with his family. You can imagine the joy of this grandfather being able to spend time with this lad, particularly since the other boys were older and too busy with other matters than to have much more than a polite relationship with their grandfather.

Not so with Joseph! He had undoubtedly heard many times about Isaac's trip up the mountain with his father Abraham to offer a sacrifice—and how God had provided that sacrifice. He heard the story often about the covenant that God had made with Abraham and Isaac.. Joseph learned at an early age that a covenant initiated by God contained an unalterable supply of grace, love, faith and provision to man. During the telling of this beautiful story and others, God was able to plant FAITH and RIGHTEOUSNESS in young Joseph that was to sustain his life in years to come!

What a unique experience Joseph had being able to, and caring about spending time with his father Jacob and his grandfather Isaac! Just imagine being only one generation removed from Abraham. There can be no doubt that Father God used these men in a powerful way to teach, train and mold the RIGHTEOUS character of the restorer Joseph. The 'Warrior Walk' of Joseph is a beautiful type of the Lord Jesus and also the remnant of Warriors that God is raising up and training in this last day.

A Mother's influence

"The rod and rebuke give wisdom,
But a child left to himself brings shame to his mother."
(Proverbs 29:15)

Rachel must have understood this principle, partly at least, from having observed the behavior of Joseph's half brothers born to Leah, Zilpah and Bilhah. This was one of the original dysfunctional blended families, but in the midst of it was righteousness. Truly Joseph never brought shame to his mother.

While Jacob and Isaac were busy teaching Joseph holy principles I believe that Rachel was instilling into him the qualities of tenderness and sensitivity. Joseph was truly a man's man as he later lived as a great faith warrior, but at the same time he could turn the other cheek and not take vengeance for himself.[7] Joseph suffered a number of injustices during his life that would have put most people in the depression basement, but there is no record that he was ever vengeful—even though it would have been considered justified to have extracted his pound of flesh.

He realized at an early age that he could not control the providential circumstances in his life, but he could control the way he responded to those circumstances!

A Holy Dream

Isaac, Jacob, and Rachel had tremendous influence on the molding of Joseph's character supernaturally. But God was busy revealing Himself to Joseph concerning a plan and a vision for the young lad's life. Joseph, being sensitive to the things of the Spirit and having 'eyes to see and ears to hear' was able to comprehend that this dream was something important from God and not just some subconscious working of the natural (carnal) mind

I have often heard that Joseph was wrong to share his dreams with his brothers because his supposed haughtiness provoked their hatred toward him. Well no doubt they hated him for sharing the dreams that revealed that they would bow to him. But their hatred toward him was because they saw in him a nature of holiness and righteousness, which brought them into conviction and condemnation. Joseph's 'love nature' revealed to them their own Unrighteousness! This pattern is repeated over and over in the scriptures and will also be true of the faithful church in this last hour as our Lord prepares His body.

The brothers of Joseph did not sell him until he was 17-years-old and that was some five years after he shared the dreams with Jacob, Rachel and the brothers.[#8] It was during those five years the brother's hatred grew toward Joseph as he would bring father Jacob the evil reports.[#9] Apparently, Jacob's family meeting had not changed the brothers' behavior and character. And as Joseph grew in righteousness he became more and more of a threat to them.

Was Joseph correct in sharing the dream? Yes! If for no other reason than to reveal to the brothers at a much later date that God had always had His hand on Joseph—and on them as well. What a joy to know that nothing is going on or happening that our Father God does not know about and has not arranged for our benefit and His glory![#10]

Should we share the dreams and visions that God gives to us? Yes and No!

Jesus said that *"You are My friends if you do whatever I command you. No longer do I call you servants, for a servant does not know what his master is doing; but I have called you friends, for all things that I heard from my Father I have made known to you"* (John 15:14-15).

I remember many years ago a young Christian who had recently been born again attended a youth conference and came home from that conference having received the baptism of the Holy Spirit along with the manifestation of speaking in tongues. He, of course, was excited at the work God had done in him and couldn't wait to tell everyone in his church about it. He immediately went to his pastor, youth pastor, a couple of elders and just about anyone that would listen to his exciting story of God's grace.

Regrettably they did not share his joy and tried to tell him he was deceived. They based that on the fact that they had not been blessed in the same way [11] and that they had been taught that those gifts of the Spirit had ended when the New Testament was completed and the early church established! This is a false theology based on experience and not on the word of God.

Wisely this young man decided to search the scriptures for himself and found that he was not the first one that had entered into this experience, and he could find no proof that God had withdrawn His spiritual gifts and left us *without* the gifts that were so important for the early church! In fact, he found just the opposite—the manifestation of speaking in tongues—occurred at least three times, and that Jesus Himself [12] had even talked about it.

Studying 1 Corinthians 14 he found what he considered the 'clincher' when the apostle Paul said in Verse 4: *"He who speaks in a tongue edifies (builds up) himself, but he who prophesies edifies (builds up) the church."* And then Paul makes this amazing statement in Verse 5a *"I wish you all spoke with tongues."* Obviously the gifts and tongues were very important, not only to Paul, but also to the early church.

The brother rightly figured if it was okay with Paul to speak in tongues and alright with the early church leaders, then it was okay for him as well. I would say that is good thinking—lining up with the word of God.

I remember the brother telling me that he needed all the help he could get—and that if praying in tongues was going to be edifying to his spiritual life then he wanted to do it! He was so funny when he said, "if those folks in the church don't need edifying that is their business, but I need all the help I can get". After all if Paul exhorted him to do it that held more sway than his home church folks who had not experienced it. They had discarded the reality of the gifts through the traditions of men [13].

Sadly the pastor and leadership of that church decided that this young man was a distraction—he was on fire for God—and they gave him the left foot of fellowship! Now many years later that young man is grown and still serving God and still on fire; while that church is just as dead as it was! Tragic! But that is what happens when you deny the power of God!

The brother shared later that if he had it to do over again that he would not have shared it with them for they did not have eyes to see or ears to hear.

Now the same was true with Joseph's family, but it was a divine necessity for him to share with his family so that many years later they would recall that God had been speaking to them, as well as to Joseph!

Endnotes: Chapter Six

#1- "Ole Salty Marine" was an endearing term used for the Marines that had been around for many years and had many experiences under the belt.

#2- Genesis 27:41 and 32:7

#3- Genesis 31:19-32

#4- Genesis chapter 34

#5- Galatians 6:7

#6- Genesis 32:26-28

#7- Matthew 5:39, Romans 12:17-21

#8- Genesis 37:10

#9- Genesis 37:2

#10- Genesis 45:5, Romans 8:18

#11- Please see endnote #1 in the 3rd chapter on 'Cessationist'

#12- Mark 7:13

#13- Matthew 15:2-20, Colossians 2:8

United States Marine Corps

THIS IS TO CERTIFY THAT

PAYNE, I. III

has faithfully given of his *time and talent to the Glory of God and the edification of Divine Services by participation in the Protestant Chapel Choir at The United States Marine Corps Recruit Depot, Parris Island, South Carolina. This certificate is given on this* eighth *day of* December *in the year of our Lord nineteen hundred and* sixty-three *in sincere appreciation of* his *contribution.*

LT COL R. N. JOBAC, USMC, Commanding Officer
Third Recruit Training Battalion

CHAPLAIN
JOHN C. HANEY JR., LT CHC USNR

100

Front Gate of Parris Island in 1963

CLOSE ORDER DRILL

Drill and the manual of arms are subjects taught throughout recruit training. Constant drilling develops teamwork and teaches instant obedience to commands.

RIFLE ISSUE

Condition of each man's rifle is recorded at time of issue and the recruit will be responsible for it during his training. Long before he fires it each recruit will be completely familiar with his M-14 rifle, inside and out.

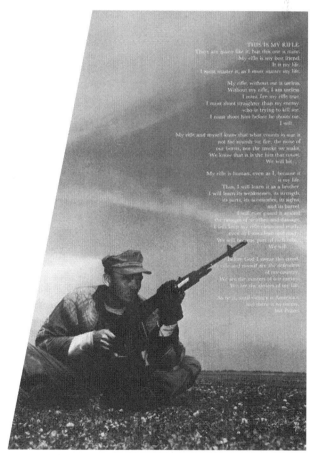

THIS IS MY RIFLE
There are many like it, but this one is mine.
My rifle is my best friend.
It is my life.
I must master it, as I must master my life.

My rifle, without me is useless.
Without my rifle, I am useless.
I must fire my rifle true.
I must shoot straighter than my enemy
who is trying to kill me.
I must shoot him before he shoots me.
I will.

My rifle and myself know that what counts in war is
not the rounds we fire, the noise of
our bursts, nor the smoke we make.
We know that it is the hits that count.
We will hit.

My rifle is human, even as I, because it
is my life.
Thus, I will learn it as a brother.
I will learn its weaknesses, its strength,
its parts, its accessories, its sights
and its barrel.
I will ever guard it against
the ravages of weather and damage.
I will keep my rifle clean and ready,
even as I am clean and ready.
We will become part of each other.
We will.

Before God I swear this creed.
My rifle and myself are the defenders
of my country.
We are the masters of our enemy.
We are the saviors of my life.

So be it, until victory is America's
and there is no enemy,
but Peace!

Training Sessions

Marksman Training

Bayonet Training

BAYONET

In this day of push-button warfare, close in fighting is still important. The bayonet and its use are a vital part of the man's combat training. Speed, balance, timing and, above all, aggressiveness make the bayonet fighter.

Obstacle
and
Confidence
Training
Course

Climbing Maneuvers

Chapel Services

...let us go into the House of The Lord

Repairing the Commander's Jeep
Ish is the one on the right

WWII - Four of the Flag Raisers (Bradley, Hayes, Sousley & Strank) appear with their jubilant buddies. Strank, Sousley and many of these boys would never make it back!
See Chapter Ten, "Occupation," to understand the spiritual concept of Matthew 12:28-29

Viet ☀ Nam Memorial Wall

Viet * Nam

The Viet * Nam Experience
"Combat Photographer"
Boston Publishing Company

1968 - Wounded and dead soldiers are evacuated by tank from Hue
(This photograph won the Robert Capa Award of the Overseas press
club). The soldier on the board is Bill *Dekker, Tom Lange's best
friend from high school. Tom volunteered to go to Viet* Nam, and
went in before Bill. Bill was drafted later. Tom was wounded in action,
and was on medical leave in San Francisco at Letterman Hospital and
while there, he found out Bill was killed and was asked to be one of
the pall bearers at his funeral. Bill was only 19 years old!

At the funeral, Bill's mother turned to Tom and asked, "Why did Bill
have to die?" Tom looked into her eyes, all along thinking he couldn't
lie, and said, "For no reason."

Graduation

Ish's Graduation Class

THIRD RECRUIT BATTALION
SGT. B.R. BRAMLETT
DEC. 4th, 1963

PLATOON 379
SGT. R.E. GREENE

M.C.R.D. PARRIS ISLAND, S.C.
SGT. J.A. FRANK
PHOTO BY I.F. MAAG

Ish's Honorable Discharge Papers
United States Marine Corps

"GOD DOES NOT GIVE US OVERCOMING LIFE,

HE GIVES US LIFE AS WE OVERCOME"

Oswald Chambers

Chapter Seven

Have You Seen?

- Have you had any dreams or visions concerning what God is doing in this hour? (Acts 2:17-27, Joel 2:28-32)

- Has the mystery of His will been made known unto you? (Ephesians 1:9-10, Romans 16:25)

- Have you been given the spirit of wisdom and revelation in the knowledge of Him? (Ephesians 1:17-23, Colossians 1:9)

- Have you seen the truth that Christ is going to be revealed in His body, which is his church? (Galatians 4:19, Ephesians 1:22-23)

- Have you seen that salvation is a walk of faith and obedience, and not just a walk to the altar? (Romans 6:4, 8:1, 1 John 1:7, 2:3-5)

- Have you seen the revelation that God is going to present to Himself a glorious church not having spot or wrinkle, but one that is holy and without blemish? (Ephesians 5:27, Colossians 1:22)

- Have you seen that the church is not one that has many denominations, schisms, divisions, but one that is characterized by 'sacrificing love?' (John 13:34-35, 1 John 2:4-6, 9-11)

- Have you seen the glory of the revealing of the sons of God? (Romans 8:19-22, 2 Corinthians 3:17-18)

- Have you seen the following? That in order to eat of the tree of life—to not be hurt by the second death—to be given the hidden manna to eat—to keep His works unto the end to receive power over the nations—to be clothed in white raiment and not have your name blotted out of the book of life—to be a pillar in His temple and have Him write upon you His new name and be granted to sit with God on His throne.

Have you seen that all of these things are required to be an **OVERCOMER**? (Revelations 2:7, 11, 17, 26 & 3:5, 12, 21)

Beloved, if you have seen any of this glory, [#1]or if you are praying to see this then read on for I believe God will reveal to you a truth that Joseph learned and exercised. When you do move in obedience to the truth you will not have to share with anyone the dreams and visions that God has shown you because they will come and ask! For they will have seen that God has become much more than just savior, baptizer, healer —they will see that He has indeed become Lord!

Now we come to the second principle that transformed Joseph's life and made him the man of character that God was able to use in a mighty warrior's way—but not without a tremendous cost!

A Warrior is 'Faithful'

Faithful is the key that Joseph learned and it is the key that brought him into the ultimate restoration and victory! Faithful is the key to *"The Warrior's Walk."*

Faithful, Faithful, Faithful! This is the key to a life of victory. Not legalistic—not religious—just faithful, faithful, faithful to the One that called you, saved you and set you apart to reveal His glory in the earth. Oh Glory! The lover of our souls has called us to partner with Him in the victory that will reveal His glory and defeat the enemy once and for all. A calling to Warriors who are willing to 'Count the cost' [#2] for the King!

Beloved, do you desire to be all that God intends for you

to be? Ask your heavenly Father to open your eyes that you might see this very clear basic truth – which is often missed because it is so simple!

Joseph was an overcomer!

Oswald Chambers said **"that God does not give us overcoming life; He gives us life as we overcome."** The trait that runs through Joseph's life is one of being "faithful" regardless of the circumstances he found himself in. Faithful—Faithful—Faithful was the key that unlocked an overcoming life for him, and being "Faithful" qualified Joseph to later be a "Restorer"! Beloved you are called to be a "Restorer"!

Faithful is a word that is kicked about quite a bit, and we generally think about it in terms of marriage—meaning that if you are married to someone you do not share your love and affections with another. Now that is certainly a correct definition, but let's look at the word "Faithful" a little closer for some meaning that I want to emphasize regarding Joseph!

Definition of Faithful:

- *"Proving oneself worthy of trust"*
- *"Trustworthy"*
- *"Long Continuance"*
- *"To be permanent and dependable"*
- *"Consistent regardless of mood or circumstances"*
- *"Dependable reliability, worthy to be believed"*
- *"Unfailing dedication and devotion"*

Certainly, all of these definitions would and should apply to marriage, but they also apply to the ***"toilet bowl brush"*** which is how I perceive that Joseph proved himself! We will look at that in a moment, but first let's look at what our Lord Jesus and the apostle Paul had to say regarding this matter of being faithful with what we have, or what we have been given.

Let's look first at Luke 16:10-12. Jesus said *"He who is faithful in what is least is faithful also in much; and he who is unjust in what is least is unjust also in much. Therefore, if you have not been faithful in the unrighteous mammon (riches), who will commit to your trust the true riches? And if you have not been faithful in what is another man's, who will give you what is your own?"*

Now let's look at this scripture and add some definitions for clarity!

*"He who is faithful (**proving oneself worthy of trust**) in what is least is faithful (**permanent and dependable**) also in much; and he who is unjust in what is least is unjust also in much. Therefore, if you have not been faithful (**trustworthy**) in the unrighteous mammon (riches) who will commit to your trust the true riches? And if you have not been faithful (**consistent regardless of mood or circumstances with unfailing dedication and devotion**) in what is another's man's, who will give you what is your own?"*

Now Paul said in 1 Corinthians 4:2, *"Moreover it is required in stewards that one be found faithful (**Dependable reliability, worthy to be believed**)."*

Looking deeper we see in Matthew 25 the way each person or steward used the talents that were given to them. It was not important how many talents they had, but how they used the talents they had been given. Those that used them wisely were told by Jesus: *"Well done, good and faithful servant; you were faithful over a few things, I will make you ruler over many things. Enter into the joy of the Lord."* You want the joy of the Lord—then the key is to be faithful! Pretty simple, just be faithful!

There was certainly no joy for those who were not considered faithful, in fact the talents they had been given were stripped from them and given to the ones that had proven to be:

- "Proving oneself worthy of trust"
- "Trustworthy"
- "Long Continuance"
- "To be permanent and dependable"
- "Consistent regardless of mood or circumstances"
- "Dependable reliability, worthy to be believed"
- "Unfailing dedication and devotion"

Remember we are looking at a *"Warrior's Walk,"* but how does this all apply to my current situation? How does Joseph who was not a warrior fit into this picture? Because he had the 'mind set' of a warrior, and that is what sustained him through many years of adversity, injustice and absolute horror.

We all know that it is easy to be *'faithful'* when everything is going to suit you and you are in comfortable surroundings. But how do we respond when things are not going our way and our flesh is crying for relief? Too often we end up having our little 'pity parties', and most often we try to recruit everyone to come to our 'pity parties' with us. For as the saying goes "misery loves company!"

How quickly in the heat of the battle do we forget the God who has called us, and promised to *"never leave us or forsake us!"*[3] The King has promised that there is a kingdom prepared before the foundation of the world for his sheep.[4] How often do we choose to wallow around in the muck of self pity, ignoring the truth that sheep are not supposed to behave like hogs! A sheep should know that his past is gone and that there is now no reason to dwell in it. His identity should be in the revelation that he has been cleansed by the blood of the lamb and he should want no more of the hog pen![5]

A sheep found in the hog pen can be assured that he got there by his own choice.[6]

You see, you can be living in a palace with servants galore and still be living a hog pen. In fact, to live under the dominion of sin and the flesh nature is to be living in the hog pen!

The sixth chapter of Romans clearly spells out the truth that you are a slave to the nature you yield to—either the nature of "righteousness" or the nature of "sin".

Now, what about the times we find ourselves in a bad place or hog-pen and we truly had no choice about it?

Joseph is such a case, but even though he found himself in horrible situations he was able to always live above them. History proved that his warrior life of overcoming in these situations was what qualified Joseph to become a ruler and a restorer. Church! Our calling is no less! We are called to **Walk as Warriors** and overcome in order that His glory is manifest!

Joseph, Prince or Slave?

Joseph by his natural birth was being prepared to be a prince. But fate and providence dealt him what would seem to be an extremely cruel and vicious blow.

When Joseph was 17-years-old his brothers, who hated him because of his righteousness and jealousy concerning the dreams God gave him, took him and were going to kill him and claim that a beast had devoured him.[7]

Reuben, Jacob's oldest son intervened to save his life and would in fact have completely rescued him and returned the young lad home. But he apparently went away for some reason and when he returned they had already sold Joseph to the Ishmaelite slave traders.

Judah also had a little mercy and decided that it was better to sell Joseph instead of killing him since he was their brother. What a nice guy!

Joseph was terrified!

The brothers had grabbed Joseph and lowered him into a cistern type pit while his cries for mercy and compassion went unheeded. Joseph probably figured his brothers were playing a cruel joke on him as they picked on him often, but soon he realized that this was no joke. They were going to kill him! We can see from later scriptures[8] that Joseph was terrified and had begged and pleaded with his brothers, but to no avail. These were cruel, violent men; seemingly without any thought or consideration as to what they were doing and the devastation they were causing to their father and family! In fact while Joseph was begging for his life the brothers sat down and had a meal that was delivered by Joseph, having been sent by their father Jacob.

Now all of a sudden, the prince, the dreamer is not under the protection of his father and his own brothers will show him no mercy!

Have you ever been afraid?

Have you ever been afraid? I mean have you ever really been terrified to the point that you could not even talk? Have you ever seen anyone in that condition? Fear is one of satan's most effective weapons and he delights in using it.

I know from personal experience as a policeman, Marine

and police chaplain involved in prison ministry what terror looks like. I have seen people that were so terrified that they could not talk and at times could not even control their body functions!

I could fill many pages with stories of crime victims and others that have experienced unbelievable terror. As a chaplain I have had men and women grab me and beg me not to leave them out of sheer fear. Prisons are one of the most fearful places on the earth and the wicked one is spiritually in charge of most of them. Why is that? Simply because a great percentage of the people in prison are under the control of satan and therefore there is a lot of demonic activity in every prison.

There is a breed of man that is almost fearless, but most people—even hardened criminals—have some sensitivity and some conscience. I believe that Joseph was a sensitive boy and therefore in the natural was subject to being terrified to the point of losing his mind. There is nothing to indicate anything in Joseph's previous 17 years that could have prepared him for what was happening to him and what was before him in Egypt.

No doubt Joseph had been the brunt of his brother's jokes and scorn (out of Jacob's hearing) for many years, but there is no indication that they had ever assaulted him prior to this time.

Can you imagine what was going through Joseph's mind as he heard his brothers negotiating his sale for 20 pieces of silver? The total desperation that he was experiencing was off the charts as he was led off to parts unknown with men even more ruthless than his brothers. We are not told about the treatment that Joseph received on the way to Egypt, but we do know that he was sold to Potiphar on the open slave market. Potiphar, the man that bought Joseph, was an officer of Pharaoh and also his chief executioner!

The prince had indeed become a slave and through no fault of his own! *And now he must become an overcomer!*

Endnotes: Chapter Seven

#1- Ephesians 1:17-18

#2- See the poem "Count the Cost" introduction to Chapter One

#3- Hebrews 13:4

#4- Matthew 25:34

#5- 2 Corinthians 5:17

#6- Joshua 24:15, Ruth 1:15-18

#7- Genesis 37:19-20

#8- Genesis 42:21, Psalms 105:17-19

No More Excuses

- ◊ Noah was a drunk
- ◊ Abraham was too old
- ◊ Isaac was a daydreamer
- ◊ Jacob was a liar
- ◊ Leah was ugly
- ◊ Joseph was abused
- ◊ Moses had a stuttering problem
- ◊ Gideon was afraid
- ◊ Samson had long hair and was a womanizer
- ◊ Rahab was a prostitute
- ◊ Jeremiah and Timothy were too young
- ◊ David was an adulterer and a murderer
- ◊ Elijah was suicidal
- ◊ Isaiah preached naked
- ◊ Jonah ran from God
- ◊ Naomi was a widow
- ◊ Job went bankrupt
- ◊ Peter denied Christ
- ◊ The disciples fell asleep while praying
- ◊ Martha worried about everything
- ◊ The Samaritan woman was divorced 5 times
- ◊ Zaccheus was too small
- ◊ Paul was too religious
- ◊ Timothy had an ulcer ....AND
- ◊ Lazarus was dead!

Now, no more excuses! God can use you if you are faithful and learn how to use...

"A TOILET BOWL BRUSH"

Chapter Eight

Toilet Bowl Brush

Where does a slave start when he has to report to work? In the lowest and worst job there is and that is where the *"toilet bowl brush"* comes in.

Can't you just see it? Joseph's first morning in Potiphar's house the chief slave comes and tells him and he will show him where he is going to be assigned. Joseph follows his new master—what choice did he have—and they go down into the bowels of the house. Joseph realizes that they are heading for the septic system, which was probably some type of water trough designed to carry the human excrement away. When they got there the chief slave opened the cleaning closet and with great pride handed Joseph a brand new *"toilet bowl brush!"*

The honcho then tells him the 'good news, bad news' story. The good news is that this brand new toilet bowl brush is Joseph's very own personal *"toilet bowl brush."* The 'bad news' is that it normally takes three men to do the cleaning, but he is going to get the honor of doing it alone, and he will not eat till he finishes!

Well, what do you suppose happened? Let me keep on painting you a picture of what I think happened.

Remember faithful Rachel. She had been faithful to him in his training and the *"toilet bowl brush"* was not new to him at all. In fact part of his training had been *'Latrine 101'* with some advance courses in *"cesspool maintenance."*

I know that as a Marine recruit at Parris Island that I was sure glad my faithful mother had trained me how to clean. My six years in military school had helped also. I know I cleaned a lot of floors with a toothbrush and wore out more than a few mops, but nothing we did could come close to comparing the jobs. Remember, they had no running water and no hot water heaters. Not to mention any flushing toilets. Just let your imagination go and you will see that this was one bad job—but someone had to do it!

But Joseph was not put off by hard unpleasant work for it had been required of him at an early age. Both Rachel and Jacob had instilled in him the proper principles of stewardship. Now he was a young slave who took great pride in performing well!

When his master showed up that afternoon to check on Joseph's progress he was pleasantly shocked to find the sewer trough was cleaner than it had ever been. He also saw that Joseph had gone on to clean other areas that had not been assigned to him. The master could never remember a young slave who had performed so well without having to be motivated,[1] it was just unheard of! The aspect that really amazed the master was that Joseph had not even complained all day about how hard the work was, how horrible and sickening the smell was—nor that it was unfair that he had to do the work of three men.

It was reported to the master by some of the other slaves that Joseph had been singing some Hebrew songs and that as he sang he had an angelic smile on his face! One of the slaves understood some Hebrew and said the songs were something like this: (Exodus 15:1-3)

> *I will sing unto the Lord, For He has triumphed gloriously!*
> *The horse and its rider*
> *He has thrown into the sea!*
> *The Lord is my strength and song*
> *And He has become my salvation;*
> *He is my God and I will praise Him;*
> *My Father's God,*
> *And I will exalt Him.*
> *The Lord is a man of war; the Lord is His name.*

129

You see Joseph's motivation was to please his Father God who he had gotten to know at an early age.

How could Joseph be so upbeat when it appeared that everything had totally come apart at the seams of his young life?

Well I believe that on the camel ride to Egypt Joseph had time to reflect on the long talks that he had with Jacob and Isaac. He recalled that God had delivered Isaac on the mountain out of an impossible situation and faith was built in him because of his early training in 'righteousness' that God would deliver him as well!

Was he recalling the dreams that God had given him? I believe that he was for the scripture says: "*Where there is no vision, the people perish.*"[#2] Joseph did have a vision that God was not through with his life, but that vision was tempered by a balance that taught him to keep his eyes on God first and the vision second. It can be a snare to dwell too heavily on the vision, for often when we do that, we try to get way ahead of where God intends for us to be at that time. It is important to let God do the work and bring to pass that which He has concerning our life. We can't rush God as much as we would like to sometimes. The sooner we come to grip with that the more joy will be manifested in our life!

Joy because we know that we are walking according to his timetable and that His intentions and plans for us[#3] are just that—His and not ours!

Jesus is the Author

To the Hebrews it is written in Chapter 12:2, "*Looking unto Jesus, the author and finisher of our faith, who for the JOY that was set before Him endured the cross, despising the shame, and has sat down at the right hand of the throne of God."* You see, if you have your eyes and faith on God He will bring the vision to pass. However, if your have your eyes and faith only on the vision, then you might miss God if He does something you are not expecting—and He is famous for that!

Joseph knew that Father God had spoken some glorious things to him. But he also knew that only Father God would be able to bring them to pass and that all Joseph could do in the interim was to be found *"Faithful"* in his current situation.

Can we do less? No! To do so is to ignore this plain and simple principle of being *"Faithful"* where we are at this very minute!

You see the scriptural facts confirm that Joseph's rise to power and authority and his warrior's walk was not because of his birthright, but because he was found *"Faithful"* in the *"toilet bowl brush"* realm!

We too have been given a glorious calling and vision, but we will not fulfill it till we also walk in the *"Faithful"* realm of the *"toilet bowl brush."*

Let's look at these facts that reveal his faithfulness. Genesis 39:2-4 says: *"The Lord was with Joseph, and he was a successful man; and he was in the house of his master the Egyptian. And his master **saw** that the Lord was with him and that the Lord made all he did to prosper in his hand. So Joseph found favor in his sight, and served him. Then he made him overseer of his house, and all that he had; he put under his authority."*

His Master "Saw"
What did his master see?

• He "saw" a young lad that had been taken from his

home and sold as a slave working and tending to things as if the house was his own!

- He "saw" that Joseph was up an hour before the bell rang worshiping his God and singing those praise songs!

- He "saw" that it didn't matter what job Joseph was assigned, he always did the job well and that he would receive correction in a spirit of humility!

- He "saw" that Joseph never complained about what others considered demeaning jobs—he was always moving in a spirit of joy—even when he had 'latrine' duty or something worse!

- He "saw" that when Joseph served at parties that he was always the neatest in his slave uniform and his master often thought *"this lad has about him a presence of royalty!"*

- He "saw" that when Joseph was sent to town to buy groceries that he could be depended on to find each item and not forget anything!

- He "saw" that when a fellow slave was sick that it was Joseph who cared for him, cleaning up after him expecting nothing in return. Rumors abounded in the slave shack that Joseph had prayed for some that were sick or hurt, and that they had been healed by Joseph's God!

- He "saw" that the other slaves loved and respected Joseph for he would often lay down his life for them, losing sleep, giving up his food, and even appearing as their advocate before the master!

- He "saw" that Joseph always moved in the established order for the household, never murmuring about the authority he was under or trying to undermine that authority!

- He "saw" no matter what Joseph was given he always got it done correctly, and he did not have to have someone always looking over his shoulder making sure it was completed!

- He "**saw**" that Joseph had proven to be a man that **could be trusted**, that he was **dependable and permanent**, that he was **consistent regardless of mood or circumstances** and that he had **unfailing devotion and dedication**. In a word Joseph was seen to be "**FAITHFUL!**"

What was the result of all that Potiphar "**saw**"? The result was that Potiphar committed everything in his house to Joseph's care! Joseph had been tested and had proven that he was a *faithful* man and a steward, first over the little things, and then after testing over the bigger things.

Beloved, Joseph did not arrive at this position of power and authority because he told Potiphar that he was *faithful*. No, he arrived in that position because he had been tested over the years and found to be *faithful*.

He proved it to Potiphar by the way he *walked* not by the way he *talked!* Joseph had learned "righteousness" as a young boy and now he had proven himself a *faithful walker* in all that he did. He was not just a *learner* he was *walker!* Glory! Praise God for the testimony set before us as an example!

Can we do less? No! Not if our vision is to walk in the footsteps of our Lord Jesus and lay down our life for His body, the church and for the healing of the nations.

I don't think for a moment that Joseph had any idea what hardships and tribulations lay before him when God shared those lofty dreams with him as a young boy. But righteousness had been so a part of his nature that he knew that the same God who spoke to him would bring it to pass regardless of the circumstances. Besides, Joseph had learned from Jacob and Isaac that things don't usually go the way you think they will as the Lord said: *"For My thoughts are not your thoughts, nor are your ways My ways."* [#4]

Joseph's confidence was in his God! If his dreams came to pass that would be just fine, but if not, he still had his God —the same God of Abraham, Isaac and Jacob! Confidence in your vision is fine. But the higher place is confidence in God and *"Dwelling in the secret place of the Most High, abiding under the shadow of the Almighty"*—Joseph could say with certainty that *"He is my refuge and my fortress; my God in Him will I trust."* [#5]

Well Joseph no longer spent his days in the latrine, but was busy running the entire household of Potiphar. It seemed as if all his preparations were close to being fulfilled, but more severe testing was right around the corner!

Soap Opera Momma

We don't even know her name, only that she was the wife of Joseph's master Potiphar, and that she started making very direct sexual appeals and enticements to Joseph.

Lust had grown in her heart to have this young *"handsomely well built"*[#6] Hebrew man who seemed to excel in everything he did.

No doubt, she had been able to seduce some of the other young men, but she was not going to be happy until she had the object of her desire which was Joseph. He was all the more of a challenge to her because he was unavailable, yet within her reach!

If she had been living in our generation (believe me she is) she would have spent her idle afternoons watching the soap operas and day dreaming about how green the grass was on the other side. The more she watched her soaps and read her love novels the more the flame of lust burned within her!

Now before you get mad at this typical, worldly, carnal woman let me state that I see her to be a type of the flesh nature that is in each of us! Yes, we are just like her if we allow our flesh to rule and reign, instead of allowing the Spirit of God to control us. You may be saying to yourself, well I am certainly not like that; but believe me you are if you subject yourself to the same mind altering and mind numbing influences that are viewed as normal by the majority of the world's population. Our Father God has made it clear *"to not be conformed to this world, but be ye transformed by the renewing of your mind."* [7]

If our mind is not consistently being renewed then we are in danger of behavior like Potiphar's wife. We must humbly remember the Apostle Paul's admonishment to the Corinthian church *"Therefore let him who thinks he stands take heed lest he fall."* [8]

To Joseph's credit and to her dismay he continued to resist[9] her advances until she decided to turn the tables on this "righteous" Hebrew. She waited until she could get Joseph alone in the house (a subtle warning) and when he again resisted her demands she grabbed his coat as he was fleeing. She then made the false claim that Joseph had come and tried to seduce her, and that when she resisted, he fled leaving behind his coat. (That is the second time a coat has caused Joseph trouble.)

When she repeated the story to Potiphar his wrath was kindled and he took Joseph and put him in prison where the king's prisoners were bound. For sure not a pleasant place! It was bad enough that Joseph was sold as a slave, now he was being imprisoned for a trumped up crime!

Righteousness or the walking in righteousness was the real reason he went to prison! The same was true throughout the history of the church for many other saints who made the choice to walk in righteousness. And will be true for many of us in this last hour before this age draws to a glorious close!

Chocolate Soldier

The heat of the battle will quickly define "*The Warrior's Walk*"!

In the heat of the battle a ferocious braggart can quickly turn into a mass of quivering jelly. But on the other hand a soldier is never really tested until he engages the enemy. The heat is the determining factor as to whether he is made of 'chocolate' and is going to melt, or whether he is made of steel that gets stronger in the fire. Joseph was definitely not a chocolate soldier! But a man of steel!

Peter said: *"Beloved, do not think it strange concerning the fiery trial which is to try you, as though some strange thing happened to you; but rejoice to the extent that you partake of the Lord's sufferings, that when HIS GLORY IS REVEALED, you may also be glad with exceeding joy."* [10] Now that's a promise! I believe that Joseph had hold of that truth and understood that what was happening to him was for God's glory—but he was going to participate as well.

Faithful in Prison

To the natural mind it looked like they had put Joseph in prison and thrown away the key. The *host of hell* was delighted that once again he had Joseph in a hard place. You can almost hear him saying, "Well, we will see what happens to our righteous Hebrew now!" Just like when they crucified the Lord of Glory and thought they were rid of him, but the tables were turned because they did not know that Father God was in control and was about to do mighty deeds of restoration.

Once again Joseph proved and demonstrated to the keeper of the prison that he was a *"Faithful"* man. We can only surmise what the conditions were like in the prison, but I am sure that they were horrible! For sure no running water, heat or air conditioning, no TV—just total misery!

Again, since Joseph was the newest prisoner and since he had made the chief executioner mad you can be assured he was not treated with kid gloves. That first morning came after a nightmarish night and he was led down those slimy stairs to the septic system. The difference was now it was under the prison and not under Potiphar's house. In order to try and make him more miserable he was ordered to leave his nice L.L. Bean waterproof boots and enter the area 'barefooted.'

He was once again given a **"toilet bowl brush"** and told there would be no food till the place sparkled!

Beloved, the older I get in the Lord the more convinced I am that the **"toilet bowl brush"** is one of the primary keys of the kingdom!

It is a simple, yet profound truth that **we will not grow spiritually past that point of testing until we have been proven 'faithful' and tested**. If Joseph had failed to use the **"toilet bowl brush"** properly he might still be down there trying to get it right. But Joseph knew in his heart that a true spiritual *"Warrior's Walk"* is only one step at a time—line upon line—precept upon precept. He knew the work had to be done in the latrine before he could progress to the shower stalls and he knew that it was not going to be pleasant.

What lessons Joseph was learning at this time are not shared with us, but we need to remember that even our Lord Jesus *"learned obedience by the things which he suffered, and having been perfected, he became the author of eternal salvation to all who obey Him"* (Hebrews 5:8-9).

It is folly to expect that we are going to enter into that which God has prepared for us without some *"learned obedience through suffering."* Don't consider that the scars you have now are the last ones you are going to receive.

The Warrior's Walk Hall of Fame

We can't forget the saints who had learned **"The Warrior's Walk"** and left us an example that has resonated throughout the history of the age!

"Tell of the likes of Rahab the harlot who received the spies in peace."

"Time would fail to tell of Gideon and Barak and Samson and Jephthah also of David and Samuel and the prophets."

- *Who through faith subdued kingdoms and stopped the mouths of lions*

- *Worked righteousness, obtained promises*

- *Quenched the violence of fire*

- *Escaped the edge of the sword*

- *Out of weakness were made strong*

- *Became valiant in battle*

- *Turned to flight the armies of aliens*

- *Women received their dead raised to life again*

- *Others were tortured, not accepting deliverance*

- *Others had trials of mocking and scourging, chains and imprisonment*

- *They were stoned and sawn in two*

- *Were tempted*

- *Slain with the sword*

- *They wandered in sheepskins and goatskins, being destitute afflicted and tormented*

OF WHOM THE WORLD WAS NOT WORTHY [11]

Beloved, the Lord said that they did not receive the promise and will not be perfected without us. Come on church, can you hear the cry? Grab that "toilet bowl brush" and let's walk as a warrior. So many have set the example for us! The cloud of witnesses are waiting for us to lay aside every weight and run, run and keep running!!

Saint, where are you?

Saints, if this teaching is making you uncomfortable, then rejoice and let us look at Romans 8:17-19 for there Paul said: *"And if children then heirs—heirs of God and joint heirs with Christ, if indeed we suffer with Him, that we may also be glorified together. For I consider the sufferings of this present time are not worthy to be compared with the glory which shall be revealed in us. For the earnest expectation of the creation eagerly waits for the revealing of the sons of God."*

So, where are you Saint?

- Are you in the cesspool of your carnal nature not yet

having learned to use the "**toilet bowl brush**" properly?

- Have you seen the vision of the glory of God, but run ahead of Him and been wrecked in the process?

- Do you find the praises of God get caught in your throat because you can see no way out of your present circumstances or condition?

- Have you realized that you had an idea of how God was going to deal with you, but it has not worked out that way, and you find yourself bitter and even mad at God?

- Have you heard a voice telling you that you will never amount to anything in God because you have made so many mistakes?

- Are you in a prison so locked up in fear that you are even afraid to talk about it?

Is there an answer? I believe with all my heart that there is for I have found myself in some of those places and when I cried out to God I heard that still small voice saying

"BE FAITHFUL!
JUST BE FAITHFUL WHERE YOU ARE"!

Praise God that He is in the delivering business, for He desires that you be free and Joseph's life proves that if you are "responsible" or "faithful" where ever you are, that God will move to bring you to the next place that He has for you —till you come to the place that Joseph did, which was to be a RESTORER!

Joseph the Restorer

Space will not allow us to look at all the details and wonderful things that happened in order to bring Joseph to the place of power in Egypt. However there is no doubt that if Joseph had failed to be *"faithful"* in the prison he would have missed God and we wouldn't be looking at his life now!

During his stay in prison Joseph remained yielded to God in his gifts and through the interpretation of dreams he was released from prison. Following his release he was able to minister to the Pharaoh—while always giving God the glory. Pharaoh decided that Joseph was the best qualified man in all of Egypt to head up the program to save them during the time of extreme famine, and Joseph did just that.

Not only did he serve as a deliverer to the people of Egypt but also to his own natural family for they now came and bowed down to him just as the dreams revealed many years before. Joseph was now 30 years old when Pharaoh put him in charge—the same age as our Lord Jesus was when he was revealed to the world to begin His ministry!

Are you Ready?

Do you see the pattern that **"God keeps his servants hidden until He is ready to reveal them—and until they are ready to be revealed,"** or until they have learned *"The Warrior's Walk!"* It takes time for our character to be molded to a place where we walk into His destiny. Often, as with Joseph it requires time in the furnace of His love to bring us to the place where *"Mercy triumphs over judgment"* [#12] and till we can "stay in the fight" till the end!

Joseph was moving in holy love and grace when he dealt with his brothers when they appeared before him. He said: *"Do not therefore be grieved or angry with yourselves because you sold me here; for God sent me here before you to preserve life. For these two years the famine has been in the land, and there are still five years in which there will be*

141

ier plowing nor harvesting. And God sent me before you reserve a remnant for you in the earth, and **to save your __ :s by a great deliverance.** *So now it was not you who sent me here, but God and He has made me father to Pharaoh and lord of all his house, and a ruler throughout all the land of Egypt."* [#13]

Church, did you hear what Joseph said? He didn't complain to them that they had sold him as a common slave and that he had been unjustly imprisoned for living a holy life. Instead he assured them that God had been in control all the time and not to be hard on themselves. What a testimony!

What a life and example is set before us! Joseph is not bitter; instead he rejoicing that God allowed him to be in a place that he might bring "**restoration**" to his family and "**deliverance**" to the world! Joseph knows and can proclaim that the God of Abraham, Isaac and Jacob is also his God and that He has engineered a mighty deliverance! He never looked back with bitterness at all his experiences, for he knew that the God who had called him had finished the work! God had found that Joseph was an honorable man that made eternal history by *"**Standing in the Gap.**"* [#14]

Joseph was a "**Faithful**" man! His respect regarding righteous responsibility reaped "**Restoration**"!

Endnotes: Chapter Eight

#1- Remember I mentioned the 'Motivation platoon" at Parris Island? Occasionally a recruit would come that was rebellious, totally insolent or just plain lazy and after working with him for a while with no positive results they would send him to the "Motivation platoon". Okay, here is how it worked: They would take you to the Motivation platoon at night usually after dark. Normally we got up at 5/5:30, but at the MP they got you up at 4:00AM. You then did one hour of push ups, pull ups and running in place. If you did that satisfactorily you were rewarded with breakfast. If not, you did it over! Breakfast consisted of one piece of white bread and all the water you could drink. Then you scrubbed the head (bathroom) with a toothbrush (usually your own) and then you went to the work yard for the day's labor. Your job was to move rocks (weighted about 30/40 lbs. each from one end of the yard to the other with a wheel barrow. The yard was about 100 yards long, and when you got to the end you dumped the rocks out, lined them up in an orderly fashion, and then went to the other end of the pile and did the same process all over again. At mid morning they would have a water break and at noon they would break for lunch. Lunch was just like breakfast—one piece of white bread and all the water you could drink.

The DI's I knew said it was amazing how quickly recruits got motivated! Usually half a day and they were ready to get with the program!

Now Joseph had no choice – probably if he did not do the assignment he would have been whipped with a *cat-o-nine* lash, or even worse!

#2- Proverbs 29:18

#3- Jeremiah 29:11

#4- Isaiah 55:8

#5- Psalm 91:1-2

#6- Genesis 39:6b

#7- Romans 12:2

#8- 1 Corinthians 10:12

#9- Genesis 39:8-10

#10- 1 Peter 4:12-13

#11- Hebrews 11:30-40

#12- James 2:13b

#13- Genesis 45:5-8

#14- Ezekiel 22:30

Honor never grows old, and honor
rejoices the heart of age.
It does so because honor is, finally, about
defending those noble and worthy things
that deserve defending,
even if it comes at a high price.
In our time, that may mean social
disapproval, public scorn, hardship,
persecution, or as always,
even death itself.
The question remains:
What is worth defending?
What is worth dying for?
What is worth living for?

William J. Bennett, lecture at United States Naval Academy,
November 24, 1997

Chapter Nine

Honor

Dateline: The North Atlantic, Dec. 19, 1943

The last time anyone saw Rabbi Alexander Goode, Methodist Rev. George Fox, Dutch Reformed Rev. Clark Poling and Father John Washington, they were standing arm-in-arm aboard the sinking USAT Dorchester, a U.S. transport ship headed to England on Feb. 3, 1943.

Shortly after midnight, the ship was torpedoed by a German submarine and chaos ensued. The four Army chaplains calmly helped soldiers and sailors into life rafts and made sure everyone had life jackets. The foursome went so far as to give up their own life vests!

In less than 30 minutes, the ship sank, leaving hundreds stranded in the icy waters off Greenland. Of the 904 men aboard only 230 were rescued.

The initial blast killed scores of men and many more were severely wounded! Quickly and quietly the four chaplains spread out among the men where they tried to calm the men knowing many would not survive.

"Witnesses of that terrible night remember hearing the four men offer prayers for the dying and encouragement for those who would live" says Wyatt R. Fox, son of Reverend Fox.

One witness, Private William B. Bednar, found himself floating in oil smeared water surrounded by dead bodies and debris. "I could hear men crying, pleading, praying," Bednar recalls. "I could also hear the chaplains preaching courage. Their voices were the only thing that kept me going."

Another sailor, Petty Officer John G. Mahoney, tried to

reenter his cabin but Rabbi Goode stopped him. Mahoney, concerned about the cold Artic air, explained he had forgotten his gloves. "Never mind," Goode responded. "I have twp pairs." The rabbi then gave the petty officer his own gloves. In retrospect, Mahoney realized that Rabbi Goode was not conveniently carrying two pairs, and that the Rabbi had decided not to leave the Dorchester.

By this time, most of the men were topside, and the chaplains opened a storage locker and began distributing life jackets. It was then that Engineer Grady Clark witnessed an astonishing sight. When there were no more lifejackets in the locker, the chaplains removed their own and gave them to four frightened young men.

"It was the finest thing I have seen or hope to see this side of heaven," said John Ladd, another survivor who saw the chaplain's selfless act.

Ladd's response is understandable. The altruistic action of the four chaplains constitutes one of the purest spiritual and ethical acts a person can make. When giving away their life jackets, Rabbi Goode did not call out for a Jew; Father Washington did not call out for a Catholic; nor did the Reverends Fox and Poling call out for a Protestant. They simply gave their life jackets to the next man in line.

Many witnesses reported that when they last saw the four chaplains they were standing arm in arm at the rail as the ship went under.

In an affidavit sent to the Army, James Ward offered his version of the last time he saw the chaplains: "They were singing songs, hymns. I knew they couldn't get off. The next time I looked the ship was slipping under the water."

"Valor is a gift", Carl Sandburg once said. "Those having it never know for sure whether they have it until the test comes."

That night Reverend Fox, Rabbi Goode, Reverend Poling and Father Washington passed life's ultimate test. In doing so, they became an enduring example of extraordinary faith, courage, selflessness and honor. [1] [2]

These men 'Stood in the Gap' for their brothers!

For me these men represent the essence of honor! They put aside their own agenda to please the one who had called them to the "Chaplaincy". And in the time of 'fire' it was revealed that these men were going to 'defend' what was important – and that defending was to save as many lives as possible. Were they worth defending? Were they worth dying for? Yes! And they did die in order that countless others would be spared to live! [3]

These men were really just regular guys, but they understood the call on their life to 'live or die' for the ones they were defending and had been called to shepherd! They understood 'honor'. And that 'honor' might require them to lay down their lives—or life jackets—but that was a small price to pay considering that their own life jacket would save the life of another.

This was not about theology or politics—it was about honor! These men were not trained as warriors, but warriors they were. Just like Joseph!

Beloved, we are exhorting one another to "*stand in the gap*" just as our Lord Jesus did when He laid down His life, not only for us, but also for the whole world. He is calling us to the same ministry in 1 John 3:16 when He said "*By this we know love, because He laid down his life for us. And we also ought to lay down our lives for the brethren.*" That is standing in the gap—to lay down your life for the brethren and all of creation. That is the revealing of the sons of God.

And when the world sees that love they will know that they are seeing the very nature of the Father, demonstrated by the Son and in the power of the Holy Spirit!

Definition of Honor

The dictionary has some wonderful definitions of honor, such as *"to promote;" "to give prestige to somebody;" "to give great respect or admiration."* But I believe that 1 Corinthians 13 defines honor with more clarity. It's the infamous "love" chapter. Let's look at it from 'The Message Bible' and use the word *"honor"* instead of *"love."* I believe you see that they are really the same.

- Honor never gives up.
- Honor cares more for others than for self.
- Honor doesn't want what it doesn't have.
- Honor doesn't strut.
- Honor doesn't have a swelled head.
- Honor doesn't force itself on others.
- Honor isn't always me first.
- Honor doesn't fly off the handle.
- Honor doesn't keep score of the sins of others.
- Honor doesn't revel when others grovel.
- Honor takes pleasure in the flowering of the truth.
- Honor puts up with anything.
- Honor trusts God always.
- Honor always looks for the best.
- Honor never looks back.
- Honor keeps going to the end.

Honor is the currency of heaven

What does that mean? I believe that it means where honor is exercised that the gates of heaven are opened and we see His glory manifested in the people, relationships and situations that we are involved in.

I really saw this demonstrated at Parris Island. I saw the DI's walking and living before us to reveal **a culture of honor that put others first**! For sure they could do anything better than we could. But the focus was for the recruits to not become just as good as the DI's—but better than the DI's. That is the heart of honor!

They taught us to *'honor one another'*[#3] and they demonstrated this as we were on our long training runs. I was fortunate because former Marines had told me "Don't go to Parris Island out of shape." Before I left the University of Tennessee I had been working out with some guys in the football weight room and I was in shape. I could do 100 push ups and 25 chin-ups as well. That was a good thing cause they loved to have you doing push ups for strength training. I also was able to run long distances without tiring.

On the second run the DI told me to fall out of the ranks and help a fellow recruit who had fallen out because he was out of shape and was 10 yards behind the platoon. He just couldn't hack it. So here I am at 155 pounds trying to help some recruit keep up who weighed over 200 pounds. But you know what it did for me? It encouraged me! I was encouraged that the DI would ask me to help and it made me want to help all the more. It was much later that I realized that they were putting us in situations where we could encourage one another and *'honor by giving preference to one another'.*[#3] They did this with every aspect of our training. They would get different ones to help those that were struggling whether it was in physical training, dismantling and cleaning weapons, memorizing general orders, chain of command or any type of protocol.

Encouragement not competition

You might not see it on the surface of the Marine combat training, but under the surface they were teaching us to 'encourage' one another to be the best that we could be.

Beloved, that is what the church and the family is also supposed to be like. I often tell people that all I want for my wife and children is **"that they may be all that God intends them to be!"** And my heart is to encourage them in their journey!

Honor always makes a decision to put love into action. And what better way to honor your loved ones than to try to bring them into all that God has for them. Why do we do that? Easy, because we know that they will find eternal joy when they find that special place that the Father has designed for them from before the foundation of the world.

Complete not Compete

If there was ever a message that I would love to get across to the church it would be **"Complete not Compete."** There is no doubt in my heart if we could get a hold of the truth to **"Complete not Compete"** that we could speed up His coming Glory.

You ever wonder why we have a gazillion different denominations. There are many reasons—some very real legitimate doctrinal issues—but many times it happens because of what I call a **kingdom building spirit**.[#4] This usually happens when ministries come to the false belief that they have a corner on some part of the gospel. And they determine that no one else should be teaching it. This is a very subtle 'religious spirit' that operates through pride, which is luciferian in nature. The wicked one is able to sidetrack the ministry and convince them that they alone have the answer. But of course that is not true. No one man or woman has the total answer.

When you see these spirits operating in either ministries or churches you know you are seeing twin religious spirits of **self-promotion and territorial preservation**. Make no mistake; these are evil spirits that desire to sabotage the work of grace and humility demonstrated by Jesus. But if we will humble ourselves and help each other be complete in what God has called us to it will be powerful. **Honor is to add our strength to another's weakness or strength**. We will never be complete without each member of the body of Christ being joined together.

The same was true in the Marine Corp. No man stood alone. He always needed the others to complete the mission. And the mission was the priority!

Every Marine was assigned an MOS [5] rating which was your specific job. But every Marine was first a rifleman. The MOS rating was 0311. This is very important in the Marine Corp for regardless what your current assignment was you were always a 'rifleman' first.

The same is true with the church. We all must be 'riflemen' first. Really it is quite simple. If you are 'born again' and have made Jesus your Lord then you are a 'rifleman.'

Your first and foremost duty is to serve the king by protecting His sheep and standing in the gap[6] for the whole body of Christ—not just your little part. That beloved is honor!

Do we have to agree with everyone to 'honor' them? No, but 'honor' them we must!

Jesus made it clear that His kingdom would be edified and seen *"if we would love one another, and that the whole world would know that we are His disciples if we love one another."* [7] Jesus did not say love only those you agree with or just those that were flowing in your particular streams, but *"to love them as He has loved you."* [8]

Vessels of honor or dishonor

"But in a great house there are not only vessels of gold and silver, but also of wood and clay, some for **honor** *and some for* **dishonor**.

Therefore if anyone cleanses himself from the latter, he will be a **vessel of honor**, *sanctified and useful for the Master, prepared for every good work"* (2 Timothy 2:20-21).

As a Christian I know we all long to hear those words of Jesus: *"Well done good and faithful servant, you were* **faithful** *over a few things, I will make you ruler over many things. Enter into the joy of the Lord"* (Matthew 25:21).

I love this scripture! If we will only be faithful! Okay, but faithful to what? To whatever He speaks to us—it is just that simple!

I remember some years ago when my friend Jason, who is a powerful young evangelist was invited to speak at a major youth rally sponsored by a large local church. The pastor told him that they were going to take up an offering and that the entire offering would go to him. The pastor cautioned him that there might not be much offering as these were teenagers mostly and they did not have a lot of money. Now Jason went and held the meetings because the Lord 'told him to go'. Jason went being obedient to the word '**Go**', and not in hopes of some big offering. That is being faithful and is honoring to the Lord who he is serving.

When the meetings were over the pastor met with Jason, thanked him and gave him the offering and told Jason that he was sorry that it was not more. Of course Jason was not complaining, because he did the meetings for his Lord, not the offering.

It was a couple of weeks later that Jason learned from two members of his family that had attended the meetings that they left generous offerings knowing that the kids did not have much money and it was their way of blessing Jason.

Jason quickly realized that just the money that his family had left in the offering (in the form of checks) was far more than the amount of the offering he received! Yikes! What does that mean? It means the pastor not only lied to him but stole from him! Not good for that pastor, for he has just become an unfaithful servant and a vessel of dishonor!

It reminds me of the story of Ananias and Sapphira!

Ananias and Sapphira

The story is told in the fifth chapter of Acts. This was during a glorious time for the early church as God was multiplying converts daily and they were moving in such love to truly share with one another. There is no doubt that Ananias and Sapphira were true believers as the cost of following Jesus was tremendous in terms of persecution and defilement by the religious community.

This couple did a generous thing by selling a piece of land and giving the proceeds to the apostles. The problem was they deceived and lied to the apostles as they had earlier connived together to keep back a part of the sales price, while claiming that the gift was the whole sales price. In other words let's say that they sold the land for $100.00, but they told the apostles they sold the land for $60.00. It was their land and no one forced them to sell it, but according to the words of Peter who said to Ananias: *"Ananias, why has satan filled your heart to lie to the Holy Spirit and keep back part of the price of the land for yourself? While it remained, was it not your own? And after it was sold, was it not in your own control? Why have you conceived this thing in your heart? You have not lied to men but to God."* [9]

At that point Ananias dropped dead! Three hours later the scene is replayed with his wife Sapphira and she too dropped dead!

You see the pastor and the church that claimed to have given Jason the whole offering did the exact same thing as Ananias and Sapphira. They deceived him in order to hold back for themselves! And that is a dangerous thing both for the pastor as well as any church staff who participated in the deception. They became vessels of dishonor! You see they could just as easily say we are going to give you "X" number of dollars for your ministry instead of twisting the truth. Scary stuff lying to the Holy Spirit!

Great fear came upon all those that heard these things realizing that lying to God and trying to deceive him is serious business.

We honor God and our brothers when we move in honesty and truthfulness, even when it is uncomfortable.

Living in your past sins is dis-honoring to God

Honor trusts God always! And that includes trusting that He has forgiven you for your past sins which have been repented for and dealt with by the blood of Jesus!

"If we confess our sins, He is faithful and just to forgive our sins and to cleanse us from all unrighteousness" (1 John 1:9).

Is He saying that if we jump through some mystical hoops He will forgive our sins? Or maybe He wants us to crawl over miles of broken glass saying some silly mantra on the way as a form of wounding ourselves for our sins. How about just drinking or drugging our sins away because the pain is just too much?

No! No! No! A gazillion times NO! Beloved, our Lord Jesus has paid the price for all our sins on the cross with His own sacrifice and blood. **And we must settle it once and for all that when we come to the Father in the name of Jesus in repentance that He forgives our sin.**

Let's look at some key scriptures to solidify this truth in your heart—for without this truth you will be living in condemnation, shame and guilt.

"As far as the east is from the west, So far has He removed our transgressions (sins) from us" (Psalm 103:12).

"But You have lovingly delivered my soul from the pit of corruption. For You have cast all my sins behind your back" (Isaiah 38:17b).

"I, even I, am He who blots out your transgressions for My own sake; And I will not remember your sins" (Isaiah 43:25).

"For I will forgive their iniquity, and their sin will I remember no more" (Jeremiah 31:34b).

Okay, some may say those are all from the old covenant, but look at this one from Hebrews where it is stated that it has been said before—meaning in Jeremiah!

"Their sins and their lawless deeds I will remember no more" (Hebrews 10:17).

Saints, He didn't just say He will forgive you. No! He said that He will remember the sin no more.

Is there something wrong with our heavenly Father's capacity to remember? Of course not! But in His sovereignty He has chosen to ***"Remember our sins no more!"***

It is upsetting when you understand how many people who are 'born again and filled with the Spirit' are living in condemnation, shame and guilt. Why are they living with this condemnation, shame and guilt? Because they don't really believe that they have been forgiven. Consequently the 'wicked one' holds it over them and causes them to lose their peace and joy.

Warriors without peace and joy will find it difficult, if not impossible to walk in victory. Only victorious warriors will go in to occupy the land for the Lord and King!

Occupation of the land is a major function of warriors, so let's take at look at what that means as I talk about it in the next chapter.

Endnotes: Chapter Nine

#1- My thanks to VFW magazine November 2008 edition for the article "Chaplains provide Spiritual Comfort on the Battlefield," by Janie Blankenship— it was invaluable. Thanks also to the "Four Chaplains Memorial Foundation" web site www.fourchaplains.org. Much of this information was obtained from their site, including the direct quotes. You can access this site for more details about these men and their families.

#2- This story is particularly dear to me as my father served on board ship—a submarine chaser—during WW2.

On my wife's side of the family her three uncles and her dad all honorably served in our armed forces.

- Her father, Airman 1st Class,Maurice Stubbs served in the Air Force in Bermuda as an air traffic controller until 1952. Following his military service he served as one of the first motorcycle policeman in Charlotte, NC.

- Her uncle, Staff Sergeant Wilburn Stubbs, served in the Marine Corps in Japan following the end of WWII.

- Her uncle Reid Stubbs served in the Air Force and flew a combat mission in a glider over Normandy on D day. He retired as a Lt. Colonel.

- Her uncle Roy Addison Stubbs was killed on board the USS Buck (DD-420) on October 9, 1943 while on an anti-sub patrol off the coast of Italy at the age of 19. A submarine had hit the USS Buck with two torpedoes and she sank within minutes leaving only 97 survivors out of the crew of 247 men. He had signed up at the age of 17 because he wanted to do his part and serve. He served honorably and 'He Gave All'!

- We are proud that our nephew Jacob Stubbs is considering joining the Air Force. He is currently serving as a 2nd Lt. in the ROTC program.

#3- Romans 12:10b

#4- A 'kingdom building spirit' is a religious spirit that blinds some leaders to the fact that there is only one kingdom and that is the *"Kingdom of our Lord and of His Christ"* Revelation 11:15b. Jesus made it clear to *"Seek first His Kingdom"* Matthew 6:33. The delusion a 'kingdom building spirit' brings is that someone's ministry is more important than our Lord's ministry. It is all too common to find ministries that are more concerned about their own personal success and reputation than the declaration of His Kingdom! When you see the spirit operating you will find spiritual abuse and manipulation at work oppressing the people. And sadly they are oblivious to what is happening!

#5- MOS stands for "Military Occupational Specialty." My MOS was first a 0311 (rifleman) and also a 3531 (motor vehicle operator). I drove 10 ton 4X trucks that were used to tow the 155mm Howitzer M1 which itself weighted 12,300lbs. I also had the privilege of being the Commanding Officer's driver. That was an honor, as he only wanted someone who was trustworthy as well as discreet.

#6- Ezekiel 22:30

#7- John 13:35

#8- John 13:34

#9- Acts 5:3

"Iwo Jima Dream"

I had a dream that I was walking with a few other guys, the only face I
remember was my friend Elliot Morales
We were enjoying the walk and I could sense a real freedom in
our countenance as we were laughing, joking around really enjoying
each other's company on a beautiful day.
But suddenly, I saw to my left a life size picture of the Marines raising the
flag on the island of Iwo Jima!
In the next moment, I seemed to come out of my body and I was watching
us walk by the picture. Then we all kind of morphed into the picture and
we were the ones placing the flag in the ground.
And clearly and loudly I heard the Lord say, "OCCUPY!"
I knew that the Lord was speaking to me about the Logan Community
through this dream. I believe He wants me to establish the
kingdom of God in that area!

Not just pray over it

Not just evangelize it.

Not just have a ministry there

But to take possession of it and set up a stronghold of God there!
"OCCUPY!"

Pastor Michael Lubanovic

159

Chapter Ten

Occupation

I was attending a pastor's luncheon when Pastor Michael [#1]asked if he could share a dream he had about the WWII battle of 'Iwo Jima'.

I had met Michael through my good friends Jason and Carmen Oberman of Strongarm Ministries[#2] as Strongarm worked closely with some of the interns at the "Fire School". Both of these brothers were deeply involved in inner city ministry and I had been thrilled at the work I had seen God do through them. Countless people have been touched as these ministries venture into the darkness bringing the light of the gospel to people that have been totally unchurched and unreached. Many of these communities they go into with the gospel are like 'third world' countries!

An Answer for me

This dream was very important to me personally as I was asking the Lord how to put the chapters together for **"The Warrior's Walk."** I knew when I heard Michael share this dream that it was part of the answer I was looking for.

You see as a former Marine the battle of Iwo Jima has a deep and significant meaning for me. I started pondering the tremendous price that was paid to **"Occupy"** Iwo Jima by the US Marines and I realized that there were spiritual parallels to the occupation that our Lord is calling us to.

The Battle for Iwo Jima

During WWII the United States was fighting the war on two completely different fronts and to lose either one would have meant a dramatic change in the destiny of our great nation! Make no mistake, the enemy was desperately trying to destroy all that we stood for and Iwo Jima was invaluable as a landing strip for our B-24s and B-29s, as well as the P-51 Mustangs. Our planes had to fly from bases on Saipan, Tinian and Guam—in the Marianas over 1,400 miles each way in order to bomb Tokyo.

Iwo Jima was currently a Japanese operated airbase capable of sending their Kamikaze fighters from Iwo Jima to bomb our bases in the Marianas Islands. Iwo Jima consisted of three different airfields, but was very barren with no potable water. As one Navy frogman asked "Why would anyone want this miserable piece of real estate?" The key was that Iwo Jima was strategically placed in such a way that whoever had it was able to exercise great military advantage. The Japanese fighter planes flying out of Iwo Jima had already successfully bombed our airfields destroying many B-29s hampering our ability to advance.

The decision was made to invade the island with the 4th & 5th division of the Marines while holding the 3rd division as a floating reserve. On the morning of February 19, 1945 30,000 Marines landed on Iwo Jima in a well coordinated invasion of this island in an operation code-named "Operation Detachment." [#4]

Some of the intelligence was flawed as the US thought that since we had been bombing this island for so long that there will be little resistance. One B-29 pilot who had flown recon flights over Iwo Jima reported that their photo interpreters saw no signs of life on the island. He reported "All you'll need is about one regiment to walk ashore and bury the dead." The fact however was as one Marine later said "The Japanese are not on the island they are in it." They had dug 11 miles of sophisticated tunnels as protective bunkers and housing, consequently there was very little sign of them.

The Japanese had turned the island into a subterranean stronghold.

For a while it looked like this invasion was not going be a big deal, but the Japanese were craftily and patiently waiting for the Marines to be gathered on the beach. Then they opened fire from strongholds including heavily fortified positions on Mount Suribachi. Carnage on the beach was the result of the devastating attacks as the Marines were trapped in the open! The Japanese were firing 650 pound shells at the beach. It didn't matter where they hit for men and machines were blown apart and sailed 100 feet in the air. The mortar type shells were so big that the Marines called the mortars "flying ash cans." They were caught totally off guard!

Keith Wheeler of the Chicago Times said in his D-day article that "There's more hell in there than I have seen in the rest of the war put together!"

Out of the nearly 70,000 Marines who landed on the beach there was a total of over 28,000 casualties, including 6,800 killed, 19,200 wounded and 2,700 suffering from total battle fatigue. Of that group there were 738 medical personnel[#3] that were either killed or wounded trying to save the lives of their brothers. They were often the first ones shot at because the enemy knew if they killed the Corpsman, fewer Marines would be saved.

Was the battle worth the tremendous cost? Yes! Following the occupation of Iwo Jima there were over 2,251 B-19s that were able to land on Iwo Jima. These were planes that were shot up, fuel starved or experiencing mechanical difficulties and could not make it back to the base in the Marianas. Each of these planes carried a crew of 12 men.

I believe the words of Charles Lindberg, the last surviving flag raiser in Mount Suribachi summed it up in these few words.

"We've got a free country. That's why Iwo Jima still matters. Japan wanted to take over the world. What we did was beat them back. Defending democracy, that's always important." [#4]

That is "**Occupation**" and you have to have occupation to have advancement!

Kingdom Occupation and Advancement!

"If I cast out demons by the Spirit of God, surely the kingdom of God has come upon you. Or how can one enter a strong man's house and plunder his goods, unless he first binds the strong man. And then he will plunder the strong man" (Matthew 12:28-29).

Jesus knew that in order for us to "Occupy" that we must first bind the strongman and render him impotent. Even though Satan was defeated at the cross and he no longer owns the earth; he is still occupying much of it. He is like the darkness that covers the surface. You only have to read the newspaper or watch the news to realize how much authority he is exercising. His goal is still as the *"thief to steal, and to kill, and to destroy."* [#5] He has much experience in the work of destruction and he exercises due diligence to bring down the Saints of the Most high God.

As you recall in Chapter Five, "**What are we fighting for?**" We saw that we were losing the war with our:

- Brothers, sisters and fellow ministers of reconciliation
- The physical and spiritual lives of our sons and daughters
- Physical abuse of our sons and daughters
- Sexual abuse of our sons and daughters
- Abortion, killing off much of our generations

These are all areas that are still being controlled by the enemy and God is calling us to occupy that land.

The goal of warfare is to fight, advance, then occupy—then fight again, then advance again to further occupy more ground. **This fighting, advancement and occupation is done over and over until the victory is secured and the enemy is destroyed!** In the process there is a dispersion of the kingdom of darkness and the establishment of His kingdom of righteousness

Occupation is a military term and God wants us to be diligent and tenacious in the advancement of his kingdom. This is not a time for wimps, but warriors!

The kingdom is not for wimps

Jesus made it clear in His testimony about John the Baptist when He said: *"From the days of John the Baptist until now the kingdom of heaven suffers violence, and the violent take it by force"* (Matthew 11:12). The Greek word here for force is "**biazo**" and it means just that: "**to use force, to force one's way into a thing**." These are desperate times and we are losing many battles. We need to change the way we think about what He has called us to. He has called us to the same calling that our Lord Jesus walked in that was clearly determined in 1 John 3:8. The powerful words *"for this purpose the Son of God was manifested, that He might destroy the works of the devil."* The enemy Satan is occupying, but he does not own. No one argues that darkness (Satan) covers the earth, but we as the body of Christ are called to co-labor with our Lord to bring His glorious light! His light will overcome all the darkness as we fight, advance and occupy!

"Put on the whole armor of God that you may be able to stand against the wiles (tricks & schemes) of the devil. For

*we do not **wrestle (Greek word—"Pale")** against flesh and blood* **(this battle is not with M-14 rifle and .45 caliber handgun, rocket launcher and grenade)**, *but against principalities, against powers, against the rulers of the darkness of this age, against spiritual hosts in the heavenly places"* (Ephesians 6:11-12). This is a spiritual battle that requires hard wrestling! It is interesting to see that this Greek word 'pale' is used only once and its meaning is clear. **It refers to warfare in general between Saints and spirit rebels who are against God and against His creation**. Hey church that's us! And that is spiritual warfare!

This is a battle that must be fought by real warriors —regardless of age—there are no limitations put on these warriors other than the limitations they put on themselves! This type of hand-to-hand combat requires training,[6] but more important it requires a tenacious determination and resolution to see His kingdom being advanced.

GO!

We see it over and over that the command from Jesus was to **"GO"**! Sometimes I think that people have misunderstood this exhortation to **"GO"** as they seem to spend all the time GOING to conventions, seminars and the like in order to learn another nugget for THEIR Christian life. And that is OK! But that is not the end, only the means to further equip you to **"GO"** and **OCCUPY**!

Don't get me wrong here. I love conferences (I am a conference speaker and teacher) and my wife Tonda and I have an agreement that we will go anywhere, anytime to sit under the anointing as we can. But only that we can be further equipped, restored and edified to **"GO"** and do His work of Occupation. Conferences and seminars are often times of wonderful restoration and renewal in order to get back in the fight! For me conferences and seminars have been instrumental in the renewing of my mind and the clarification of who I am on Christ! And that's big!

Going means different things to different people and we have to be careful not to put people in a box of our own calling or thinking. What going means to me may not be the way He is calling you at all. But He is calling you to **"GO"**!

Your **"GO"** may be having a love of people, and the ability to share His love in a "coffee shop" setting. Or it may be like my dear friends Darlene and Fred Pitts[#7] who labor in a neighborhood in South Carolina that has been described as a "third world neighborhood" sitting a mile from affluent homes. Many of the houses Darlene and Fred go into don't even have running water or bathroom facilities! Darlene and Fred are shining lights in gross darkness and they have chosen to **"GO"** and occupy the land!

Jesus said to **"GO"** to the original twelve: *"As you **go**, preach, saying; the Kingdom of heaven is at hand. Heal the sick, cleanse the lepers, and raise the dead, cast out demons. Freely you have received, freely give"* (Matthew 10:7-8).

To the seventy Jesus said: *"**Go** your way; behold, I send you out as lambs among wolves. And heal the sick there, and say to them, the Kingdom of God has come near to you"* (Luke 10:3 & 9).

And of course the Great Commission: *"Jesus came and spoke to them, saying, All authority has been given to me in heaven and on earth. **Go** therefore and make disciples of all nations, baptizing them in the name of the Father and of the Son and of the Holy Spirit. Teaching them to observe all things that I have commanded you; and lo, I am with you always, even to the end of the age"* (Matthew 28:18-20).

Can we lose the war?

Yes! We can lose the war by "imploding". Implosion is defeating us by refusing to recognize the enemy and his pernicious purpose for our lives. We have got to really dig in and fight!

Frankly I am appalled at the depth of ignorance and lackadaisical attitude in churches concerning spiritual warfare. And the ignorance is certainly across the denominational lines as well as those claiming to be independent. Very few churches really have a grip on what the enemy is doing. And fewer still are standing on the wall or in the gap to fight!

We are like the recon missions at Iwo Jima that said, "don't worry you only have to go in and bury their dead." In a final analysis of the battle of Iwo Jima it became apparent that the US underestimated the strength of the enemy by at least 70%. Further it was evident that the enemy had dug in deep and had established strongholds[8] that were not going to be easily removed. It reminds us that before we go to engage the enemy we had better be in prayer and ready to do battle with an enemy that is determined. You see the devil may occupy the land but he does not own it. Jesus owns it as He bought it back at the cross! The deed was signed with His own blood!

That faulty recon on Iwo Jima cost the lives of over 6,800 men and countless other casualties.

Let's look at some statistics[9] about what people think about the reality of Satan. It is very interesting as the statistics look at different groups including the totally unchurched.

◊ Unchurched – 64% say that Satan is not a living being, but is just an evil symbol.

◊ Born Again Christians – 46% deny even the existence of satan.

◊ Catholics – 64% say that the devil is non-existent and only a symbol of evil today.

◊ Americans in general – 57% say that the devil is not a living being, but only a symbol of evil today.

No wonder we are in so much trouble! The difference between these people groups is minimal. And it reveals that we have been badly deceived or blinded by the very one that supposedly does not even exist.

The Bible is very clear that the devil, satan, the wicked one or whatever name you choose to call him is very alive and doing his destructive work on the earth and in all of creation. How can the church battle him if they don't even believe he exists? You won't fight if you don't know there is a battle going on. In fact if you don't know there is a battle— and you are not fighting—then you have already lost!

Okay, let's look at some scriptures that prove that satan is busy about being destructive.

◊ *"The **thief** comes only in order that he may steal and kill and destroy"* (John 10:10 AMP).

◊ *"To keep **satan** from getting the advantage over us; for we are not ignorant of his wiles and intentions"* 2 Corinthians 2:11 AMP).

◊ *"For we wanted to come to you, I Paul, more than once, and yet **satan** thwarted us"* (1 Thessalonians 2:18 NAS).

◊ *"Be of sober spirit, be on the alert. Your adversary, the **devil**, prowls about like a roaring lion, seeking someone to devour"* (1 Peter 5:8 NAS).

◊ *"You know of Jesus of Nazareth, how God anointed Him with the Holy Spirit and with power, and how He went about doing good, and healing all who were oppressed by the **devil**; for God was with Him"* (Acts 10:38 NAS).

Warriors! Do you hear the trumpet sound? Are you ready to lift your sword to fight? Can we be the generation that clearly hears the clarion call to step up and stand against the darkness wherever we find it? Yes warriors we can! He has called us to labor with Him in healing those that are oppressed, wounded and captured. He has given us the same Holy Spirit that raised Jesus from the dead and He desires that we do even greater works than He did.[#10] Does that seem unnatural? Well it is, because those works are supernatural and that is **"The Warrior's Walk"**—doing those supernatural works that are setting creation free from the *"bondage of corruption into the glorious liberty of the children of God."* [#11]

For the battle to be won we must have trained and tested "Watchman Warriors" that are able to stand and demonstrate by their lives how to walk as The Warrior!

Leaders are not born, they are discipled!

"Leaders are not born, they are discipled!" [#12] Do you know what the difference is between a disciple and a student? The answer is simple, yet profound and life changing when you are being discipled by the right Master. A student learns what his teacher knows, but a disciple becomes what his Master is.

In our next chapter let's look at this tested warrior—one who is being discipled by the Master!

Endnotes: Chapter Ten

#1- Pastor Michael Lubanovic is the outreach pastor for The Fire School & Church www.Fire-school.org

#2- Jason and Carmen Oberman are the founders and directors of Strongarm Ministries www.strongarm.org

#3- My friend Samuel Russell McGee, III was a corpsman attached to the Marines in Viet Nam. He was killed by small arms fire (direct shot to the chest) while serving in the Quang Nam province on June 9th, 1967. He and I graduated from military school in the same class of '62

#4- A lot of my research came from what I learned at Parris Island as a young recruit, but I want to thank Donald L. Miller for his wonderful article "Deathtrap Island" that appeared in the magazine "Iwo Jima" published by Weider History Group, 741 Miller Drive SE, Suite D-2, Leesburg, VA 20175-8994 (703) 771-9400

It was exciting that I 'just happened' to find this magazine within a week of Michael sharing his dream on Iwo Jima. I love God's timing!

#5- John 10:10

#6- I love this little story, but I would not recommend that you emulate it in the classroom!

Three things you need to keep in mind before you read this story.

1. Marines are taught and trained to protect and honor

2. Marines are taught to keep your priorities in order

3. Marines are taught to know when to act without hesitation

A Marine was attending college courses between missions in Iraq and Afghanistan. The professor, an avowed atheist, shocked the class one day when he walked in, looked toward the ceiling, and said loudly. "God if you are real, then I want you to knock me off this platform. I'll give you exactly 15 minutes."

The room fell silent and the professor began his lecture. Ten minutes went by and the professor proclaimed, "Here I am God still waiting."

It got down to the last minute when the Marine stood up, walked toward the professor and threw his best punch knocking him off the platform and out cold. The Marine went calmly back to his seat and sat down. The other students were shocked and stunned and sat there looking on in silence. The professor came to, noticeably shaken, looked at the Marine and asked, "What the heck is the matter with you? Why did you do that?"

The Marine calmly replied, "God is busy today protecting America's soldiers who are protecting your right to behave like an idiot and say stupid stuff. So He sent me!"

#7- Darlene is the founder and director of Power Team Inc., an inner-city ministry reaching hundreds of children and adults with the love of Jesus. Her husband Fred also serves with her in the trenches. They can be reached at Power Team Inc., www.powerteaminc.org

#8- For a clearer understanding of the spiritual dynamics of "Strongholds" check out my book "Life in the Red Zone", Chapter 1.this can be ordered from www.restoringhearts.net

#9- The Barna Group, www.barna.org

#10- Romans 8:11, John 14:12

#11- Romans 8:21

#12- Keith & Sodonia Genteman coined this quote "Leaders are not born, they are discipled," while student teaching on discipleship at Zion College Ministry Training Center www.Zioncollege.com.

The LORD reigns, let the earth rejoice;
Let the many islands be glad.
Clouds and darkness surround Him;
Righteousness and justice are the foundation of
His throne.
Fire goes before Him
And burns up his adversaries round about.
His lightnings lit up the world;
The earth saw and trembled.
The mountains melted like wax at the presence
of the Lord,
At the presence of the Lord of the whole earth.
The heavens declare His righteousness,
And all the peoples have seen His glory

Psalm 97:1-6 NASB

Chapter Eleven

Watchman on the Wall

Dateline: December 1963: Parris Island, SC, Marine Corps Training Division.

Sgt. Green, my senior drill instructor was pacing up and down the squad bay as he was giving us final words of encouragement and exhortation before we were to be shipped out the following day to Camp Geiger for "advanced combat training." Tomorrow was a big day—the biggest ever—for now after 12 weeks of intense boot camp at Parris Island we would finally be referred to as Marines, not just recruits!

"Men, your life will never be the same, for now you have proven to us that you want to be a part of the best; for only the best make it this far. Your training, however is not over, in fact it is only beginning if you want to stay the best. You have been *safe here at Parris Island*, but you won't be safe if you go 'in country, the country of living hell' (referring to Viet Nam) where not only the bullets and the RPG's will kill you, but the landmines, poisoned rat holes and snake snares will kill, maim and cripple you. *If you have not learned to hear the voice of authority here and to respond to that voice you will not only get hurt, but you will be a hazard to every other Marine in your unit.*"

It was pitch dark in the squad bay, and we were already in our bunks with the lights out. But because the full moon was shining in the windows I could see Sgt. Green's face as he walked by. Suddenly I realized that the Sgt. had big tears running down his face—what a surprise—I honestly did not think this man was capable of emotion, much less tears. But there he was crying. Then it hit me—he was crying for us! Yes! He was crying for us! This man who had made us do 1,000's of push ups, run 100's of miles and "thumped

173

us" (we were part of the old Marine Corps) over every minor infraction—from a uniform wrinkle to scratching a sand flea was crying *because he loved us and he had the heart of a shepherd for us!* Yes, the heart of a shepherd. He knew that many of us would go "in country" and if we had paid attention in training and to his voice then we had a better chance of survival. He knew he was at least partially responsible for us as he had taught us to co-labor with those in authority, and to honor them because of their experience and the price they had already paid!

Just as the Marine Corps gave me drill instructors to hone and perfect the skills of a warrior, my Heavenly Father has given unto His church the fivefold ministry to equip the saints for the work (battle) of taking and occupying the land!

What is a Watchman?

A watchman is one who is called, commissioned, has been trained, tested under fire, faithful and will do anything possible to guard and carry his sheep. In other words he is willing as Jesus was to lay down his life for the sheep[#1] as well as for those not yet in the sheep fold.

What are the key words here?

- Called
- Trained
- Tested under fire
- Faithful
- Guard
- Carry
- Lay down life

Called and Trained

In the Marine Corps the DI's are volunteers that have asked to be further trained and hardened in order that they can then do the same for recruits. For them it is a **calling**. They take it very seriously and many of them wash out of the DI training. The strenuous demand of the DI training is the reason that they are so prepared for the training of the recruits.

The same is true of the **calling** of a watchman or shepherd. They must first be **trained**. Often in America we think of ministry training as attending a seminary, bible school or some other theological institution. These institutions can certainly help and educate you, but they will not necessarily prepare you. Spiritual education and spiritual preparation are two very different things!

Education will give you head knowledge, but preparation will give you experience knowledge. They are two totally different things. An example would be the life of the early apostles such as James, John and Peter. They had no formal theological education, but they were trained by the Master himself and they experienced the revelation and reality that He was teaching. Those brothers were busy about doing the work of the Kingdom, which was healing the sick, teaching, casting out demons and doing many other signs and wonders. They learned by being a disciple of the Master. Their theological class room was walking with Jesus! They just didn't have head knowledge, they had experience knowledge! They knew the Master, not just about Him. Do you see the difference?

On the other hand, we have the apostle Paul, who was highly educated and after his conversion on the way to persecute Christians[2] he became a powerful ministry. He not only left us with many epistles, but an example of how we are to live and walk as a Warrior. Paul had the balance, but it came through experience – truly the **school of hard knocks**.

There is nothing wrong with Bible schools and seminaries if they are teaching and mentoring you in the ways of Jesus![#3] A watchmen must know God; not just know about Him. Paul said: *"That I may know Him and the power of His resurrection and the fellowship of His sufferings, being conformed to His death"* (Philippians 3:10). Don't waste you time and money attending a school that will only give you head knowledge. You will surely end up disappointed and discouraged. The gospel of the Kingdom is one of power. And we have a responsibility as Christians to reveal that power!

Remember our job description that is found in Matthew 10:7-8? *"And as you GO, preach, saying; The Kingdom is at hand. Heal the sick, cleanse the lepers, and raise the dead,[#4] cast out demons. Freely you have received, freely give."*

Notice! Preach is only the first thing. If your Bible school, seminary or other theological institution is not teaching and imparting the solid truths of healing the sick, cleansing the leper, raising the dead, and casting out demons then find another school!

Tested under fire - Not Chocolate Warriors

Talking about leaders the apostle Paul says: *"He must not be a recent convert, or he may become conceited and fall under the same judgment as the devil. He must also have a good reputation with outsiders, so that he will not fall into disgrace and into the devil's trap"* (1 Timothy 3:6-7).

Why is the apostle Paul giving the message to the young Pastor Timothy? Paul knows that conversion is a powerful thing and that the converted are so excited that they feel like they can take on the world, the flesh and the devil. But the truth is they are not ready! They must be trained and they must be tested. There are no short cuts to this process and many folks are ship wrecked by trying to circumvent the **character building process.**

We have all seen this happen countless times. Many are the famous athletes who had an experience with God and their fans are so excited they set up opportunities for them to share their testimony; sometimes with thousands of people in attendance and often on television. Then they experience a major *"Whoops"* and their testimony is wrecked and often they are as well. And of course many other folks are damaged and the testimony of God's love and grace is set back. All because they were not trained and tested.

Even sadder are the stories of the untested pastors and evangelists that get wrecked because the **character building process** has not been brought to maturity. They have the precepts, the principles, the intellectual understanding, the degrees; but they have not been tested. And in the fire they melt and slime all over themselves and other folks. Not a pretty sight!

The Marine Corps DI's that trained me for combat were all tested men that had proven their mettle. These were men of strength, honor and integrity and you could follow them into the fires of hell knowing they were leading the charge! These men were not Chocolate Warriors! They had been proven and tested many times, and were hard battle veterans.

I want to follow a ministry (whether male or female) that understands hand to hand combat with the forces of hell and is not squeamish to swing the sword of the Spirit to bring healing and deliverance. I also want to know that they have my back and will give their life for me. That is spiritual warfare. Beloved we are not talking here about natural warfare, but spiritual warfare. Most of these warriors will never look like the **Hulk** or be engaged in ferocious fire fights. But they will be a spiritual **Hulk** and the demons of hell will run from them! Yes run from them!

This kind of authority and power does not come because we ask for it, but rather we are trained and tested in it. Oh we can ask for it, but believe me when you do the testing will begin. Why? The **Master DI** wants to see if you are seriously made of spiritual steel or chocolate.

Everybody wants to preach, but who wants to clean the toilet?

Remember the story of Joseph and the *"toilet bowl brush"?* It was the toilet bowl brush that was used to train his character. And it was also used to see if he had passed the test.

I recall as a pastor in charge of a large training program where we taught ministry schools a number of dear people came and told me they were called to be ministries such as pastor, evangelist and teacher. They wanted me to teach them how to do it and always expressed their excitement at the prospect of standing before the people and expounding His word. At the time I was teaching and ministering sometimes 7 days a week so I would tell them to meet me the next morning at the church at 6:30am. They would always respond with something like, "Oh great we are going to get there early to pray together." "No" I said, "pray before you get there; for at 6:30 we have to prepare for the day of teaching and ministry." And then I added, "And come prepared to walk with me through the day till about 11:00pm." Interestingly most never even showed up.

Out of the ones that did show up only a few made it through the day. We would start by checking all the bathrooms and cleaning up where necessary. Then we would gather the music for the morning's sessions and make sure the sound board was tested and working properly. Of course when you have 100 people at a school there are always many fires to deal with and put out and the issues start early. And being in charge meant you had to do it, whether it was cleaning the toilet, washing dishes, teaching or casting out demons. It is all part of being a pastor/teaching ministry. Some would never show up. Some would stay for half the day. Some would stay for the whole day and then never come back. But some passed the test of service and became real warriors fighting in the trenches on the front lines!

The most frequent question or statement was "I am not really interesting in doing all this stuff I just want to pastor or teach." I would respond with something like "well then the pastoral/teaching ministry is not for you. All true ministries are service! And more important is the Walk you have before the people. They can hear you preach and it might be anointed and powerful, but if you don't have an anointed and powerful walk of love and service it is only a noisy gong or clanging cymbal."[#5]

It is still about Character

"Who, then, is the man that fears the LORD? He will instruct him in the way chosen for him. He will spend his days in prosperity, and his descendants will inherit the land. The LORD confides in those that fear Him; He makes his covenant known to him" (Psalm 25:12-14).

The apostolic minister Derek Prince said the following regarding this scripture in the Psalms.[#6]

"It is important to understand that God chooses his pupils primarily on the basis of character, not intellectual attainment, not academic degrees, not social privilege, but on the basis of their heart attitude toward Him. He looks for a man who fears the Lord, who has reverent respect and fear for the Lord. He says such a man He will instruct in the way chosen for him. Such a man will spend his days in prosperity; his descendants will inherit the land.

Then He goes on to say something even more wonderful: "The Lord confides in those who fear Him." Another translation says, "The secret of the Lord is with those who fear Him." I think there is no greater privilege in our relationship with another person than when that person comes to such a place of confidence that he'll share his secrets with us. And it really staggers me to think that if we have that attitude of reverent fear toward the Lord He'll even share His secrets with us and He'll make known His covenant to us.

You see, all of God's blessings are based upon His covenant and when He makes known His covenant to us then it opens the way to enter into all the blessings which God has provided."   --Derek Prince

We have already looked at the life of Joseph and saw that it was at least 12 years before he passed the character test and was ready to be a true Watchman or shepherd.

Beloved, don't get in too big a hurry. We are eternal and the work God wants to do is an eternal work and it takes time to get us ready. It is the hardest thing to rest and wait, but it is necessary for His plan to be unfolded in your life. Hold on to this promise as you walk with the King. *"Those who wait on the Lord shall renew their strength; they shall mount up with wings like eagles, they shall run and not be weary, they shall walk and not faint"* (Isaiah 40:31).

Faithful

Again the story of Joseph is our proof text to show how important Faithfulness is to God!

Faithfulness draws the favor of God whether it is in a

job, marriage, hobby or His Kingdom work. This was certainly true in the military. No one joined up and became a general in the same day. No, not even close although it was obvious that many thought they should be.

My dear friend and fellow warrior, Pastor Wayne Clarke didn't just join the Navy and become the Commanding Officer of the USS Dolphin, a record breaking deep diving submarine. No! He paid his dues and was sorely tested long before he entered the US Naval Academy. Following his graduation from the Naval Academy he worked his way up through the ranks being tested, tried and found faithful before he was given the Command of the USS Dolphin. Along the way of his path in the Navy he was trained in all types of submarines and served on diesel powered subs as well as nuclear powered Poseidon Missile submarines.

Why did our brother Wayne end up being the Commander when there were other men that were just as qualified? Because along his career he proved to those in authority that he was faithful and he had the resolve to fight the fight!

And what leaders look for is faithfulness and a resolve to fight!

To be in authority you must be under authority

You see to be **in authority you must first be under authority!** This military principle was learned from the scriptural principle revealed over and over in the Bible! It is also true in every aspect of life.

This is such an important truth in His Kingdom that those who understand it and move in it will enjoy His favor. Those that don't understand it will have a hard time and be confused most of the time. They will constantly be trying to earn a place of authority, never understanding that authority only comes through submission. Peace comes from order. And order comes through the Father's authority. Peace and authority come from submission to the authority that has been placed above you.

Remember Joseph, our example? He proved to those in authority over him that he was a faithful man!

Was the authority over him in Potiphar's house righteous? Was the keeper of the prison righteous? We don't know, but probably not. But Joseph honored them and submitted to their authority and he gained their favor when they **saw** his walk before the people.

When Joseph came into a place of ultimate authority he moved in love and mercy for he had seen both the righteous authority and the unrighteous authority.

Wolves in sheep's clothing

"His Watchmen are blind,
All of them know nothing.
All of them are mute dogs unable to bark,
Dreamers lying down, who love to slumber;
And the dogs are greedy, they are not satisfied
And they are shepherds who have no understanding;
They all have turned to their own way,
Each one to his unjust gain, to the last one."
Isaiah 56:10-11 NASB.

These are certainly not words that were meant to compliment! Rather they were stinging words revealing our Lord's grave displeasure at the hearts and lives of some watchmen and shepherds.

These watchmen and shepherds were not guarding and carrying the sheep. Instead they were abusing the sheep and taking advantage of them at every opportunity. They were using the sheep to feed their own appetites and egos. These shepherds are too busy with their own agenda to take care of the sheep. They generally have the **kingdom building spirit** [7]talked about in chapter nine.

While it is not fun to look at the negative that is happening among some watchmen and shepherds, it is necessary to discern the evil from the good. I am frequently asked how you can discern the wolves from the true shepherds.

Here are a few things to look for that would be indicators that there are serious problems.

- Does the shepherd exaggerate?

- Who are they really accountable to? Every ministry needs outside independent counselors and not just "yes" men.

- Are they trying to hide money?

- Who does their accounting and is it open for you to see?

- Do the shepherds have time for their own sheep?

- Do they handle confrontation with honor?

- Do they release the sheep to graze in other conference pastures without being in fear?

- Are they trying to control or manipulate your life through legalism or fear?

- Do they confront sin in love, but at the same time deal with it?

- Do they teach you that relationship with God is more important than rules?

When you see these attitudes and behaviors being manifested, go to the Father, pray and ask for discernment. He has promised to give you discernment. *"For the word of God is living and powerful, and sharper than any two edged sword, piercing even to the division of the soul and spirit, and of joints and marrow, and is a **discerner** of the thoughts and intents of the heart"* (Hebrews 4:12).

I think Billy Graham has given the church and ministries a wonderful example to follow which is to *"avoid every appearance of evil."* [8] For sure that lifestyle shuts the mouth of the devil every time!

Guard, Carry and Lay down life

These are all traits that you will find in the true shepherd for they are indeed followers of the Chief Shepherd the Lord Jesus!

Remember when Jesus told the story of the shepherd leaving the 99 and going after the one? At that moment the one was lost [9] and the shepherd could not rest until he was safe. That is the heart of a true shepherd! Not only did the shepherd find the sheep, he carried him back home on his shoulders. Do you see the power of this story? Beloved, our chief Shepherd will do whatever is necessary to redeem us, restore us and return us to our rightful home which is in Him!

Paul writing to the Thessalonians said *"Comfort the fainthearted, uphold the weak, be patient to all."* [10] He also said similar words to the Roman church *"We then who are strong ought to bear with the weaknesses of the weak, and not to please ourselves."* [11]

Sheep, Wolf, or Sheepdog!

Sgt. Jeff Johnson of the Colorado Springs Police Department said, "When Matthew Murray entered the New Life Church with 7,000 worshipers inside, he had already killed four people and wounded five others."

Jeanne Assam, a church member who served as armed security for the church, heard the shots and ran toward the scene. She saw the gunman who was armed with an assault rifle, two handguns and hundreds of rounds of ammunition. By the time he entered the church he had already attacked a family in the church parking lot killing sisters Rachel, 16 and Stephanie, 18, and severely wounding their father David Works.

Some 12 hours earlier Murray had killed two staff members at the "Youth with a Mission" training center 80 miles away in Arvada, Colorado. Killed during that attack were Tiffany Johnson, 26, and Philip Crouse, 24. Also, two other staff members were shot and one was in critical condition.

Jeanne had been trained to shoot as a police officer. However, the important thing during this unwarranted attack was that she had "**Resolve**" to end the situation and not let any more be hurt or killed if she could prevent it.

She knew she had to be a **Sheepdog** for a **Wolf** was loose destroying the **Sheep**!

Not being concerned for her own safety she started towards Murray demanding that he drop his weapon and when he did not respond she discharged her weapon, killing him instantly. She later said, **"I saw him coming through the doors. I took cover and waited for him to get closer, and I came out of cover (she was totally exposed), identified myself, and engaged him and took him down."**

Senior Pastor Brady Boyd said, "She probably saved over 100 lives today. If the gunman had gotten another 60 feet no telling how many would have died."

The following statement by Jeanne sums up what a **"sheepdog is to the wolf."** She said, **"I did not run away and I didn't think for a minute to run away. I just knew that I was given the assignment to end this before it got too much worse. I just prayed for the Holy Spirit to guide me. I was just finishing a three day fast and was very weak, but my God was strong."**

Another church member a Viet ✳Nam vet was also at the church, but in the cafeteria when he heard the shots. He ran toward the shots as the rest of the people were scrambling in all directions. When he arrived he saw Murray dressed totally in black firing wildly in all directions and headed for the sanctuary. The Viet ✳ Nam combat veteran, saw another guard standing with his gun drawn, but the guard was frozen and unable to fire his weapon. The vet called out "Gimme your gun. I've been in combat. I am going to take this guy out." The guard was too frozen to respond even though the combat vet said it many times. The vet then came out from behind the pillar without a weapon and advanced toward the shooter calling him a coward, trying to draw his attention away from the other people. Jeanne showed up at that moment and advanced on the shooter at the same time. The difference was she had a gun and used it to take him down! [#12]

Both of these folks were sheepdogs having the resolve and the training to take the wolf down. The other guard, although armed, was totally ineffective in the fight. He was not a warrior, but a **"chocolate soldier."**

Jeanne's resolve has to be our attitude as we engage in spiritual warfare with the enemy! When we see the enemy at work we need to come out of cover—identify ourselves—engage him—and take him down!

Church, that is what standing on the wall and in the gap is all about! Most of us won't be in the position that Jeanne Assam found herself in that tragic day, but if we are not trained, tested, faithful, willing to carry and guard the sheep and ultimately lay down our life for the sheep—then we will never **"Walk"** into our destiny as a **"Warrior!"**

Endnotes: Chapter Eleven

#1- John 10:11, Isaiah 40:11

#2- Acts Chapter 9

#3- There are many wonderful ministry schools in America. I could certainly recommend the following schools that will give you both intellectual understanding and supernatural ministry experience as well. You will then be prepared and trained to GO into the fields that are white for harvest.

- Zion College, Fort Mill, SC www.Zioncollege.com.

- The Fire School of Ministry, Harrisburg, NC www.fire-school. org.

- Morningstar Ministries, Fort Mill, SC www.morningministries. org

- Bethel School of Ministry, Redding, CA and Atlanta, GA www. ibethel.org & www.ibethelatlanta.org.

- Global School of Supernatural Ministry www.globalawakening. com; Mechanicsburg, PA.

#4- Rolland and Heidi Baker www.iris.org while serving as missionaries to the people of Mozambique have seen miracle after miracle as God reveals His love. Blind eyes are opened on a regular basis and over 100 folks have been raised from the dead!

Also there have been many confirmed people raised from the dead in Mexico. You can find some of these testimonies (over 400 people raised from the dead) at the web site of David Hogan an evangelist to the wilds of Mexico. www.freedom-ministries.us

I mentioned the book "Mega Shift in the end note for chapter one and again I would refer to it for many examples of people being raised from the dead along with confirmation. Information can be found at www. megashift.org.

Many people ask "If God is raising people from the dead why are we not seeing it happen in the US. For me the answer is simple. The prevalent "Culture of Doubt" prevents many miracles from taking place!

#5- 1 Corinthians 13:1

#6- This quote taken from "A Word from the Word" radio archives by Derek Prince. The title of this article is "From Enrollment to Graduation", used with permission from Derek Prince Ministries, www.DerekPrince.org

#7- An explanation is given of "kingdom building spirit" in the end note #4 at the end of Chapter 9.

#8- 1 Thessalonians 5:22

#9- Luke 15:4-7

#10- 1 Thessalonians 5:14b

#11- Romans 15:1

#12- Material selected from articles on the web at:

www.TheDenverChannel.com, www.cnn.com, and www.RockyMountainNews.com., www.msnbc.com

A Fight to the Finish

"And that about wraps it up. God is strong, and He wants you strong. So take everything the Master has set out for you, well-made weapons of the best materials. And put them to use so you will be able to stand up to everything the Devil throws your way. This is no afternoon athletic contest that we'll walk away from and forget about in a couple of hours. This is for keeps; a life and death fight to the finish against the Devil and all of his angels.

Be prepared. You're up against far more that you can handle on your own. Take all the help you can get, every weapon God has issued, so that when it's all over but the shouting you'll still be on your feet.

Truth, righteousness, peace, faith and salvation are more than words. Learn how to apply them. You'll need them throughout your life. God's word is an indispensable weapon. In the same way, prayer is essential in this ongoing warfare. Pray hard and long. Pray for your brothers and sisters. Keep your eyes open. Keep other's spirits up so that no one falls behind or drops out."

Ephesians 6:11-13 MSG

Chapter Twelve

It's a Love War

It was a wonderful day when I left Parris Island and was finally called a Marine. No longer was I just called a recruit. I knew that I had accomplished something special that would have a lasting impact on my life.

But what I didn't understand at the time was that my training was just starting and would continue for many years, both as a Marine and as a Spiritual Warrior. The training for Spiritual Warriors never ends this side of the veil as our Lord desires to take us deeper and deeper into His purposes for His Kingdom.

During the time I was at Parris Island I didn't have a clue that the Lord was going to reveal what He was doing in my life as well as the Body of Christ. This book is the result of what I learned about the correlation between my training as a **Combat Marine** and a **Spiritual Warrior.**

The fight is always between light and darkness and we have to be trained to overcome the darkness and walk in the light. Truly the spiritual war is fought with spiritual weapons, but the greatest weapon of all—is LOVE! It is a Love War.

Light overcoming darkness

It is undeniable that darkness is nothing more than the absence of light. Mr. Webster defines darkness as "entirely or partly without light."

Well the same is true with spiritual darkness—it is an area that is "entirely or partly without light."

There is no doubt much of the entire world is still living

in darkness! Spiritual darkness is prevalent throughout. The reason is that the Light[#1] is not shining bright enough to be seen and followed in this hour. The light of His oil has gone out in many places and in many places there is no oil at all.

Beloved, the Church His Bride, the Body of Christ is His light and we need to be shining brightly wherever we are. He is the head and we are the body. We are supposed to be reflecting His life in our life.

John Paul Jackson[#2] told a story about being in Salem, Massachusetts the week before Halloween when there is a gathering of 400,000 witches' celebrating the pagan holiday. In his words he said, "What a great place to show the love, power, and grace of our Lord Jesus in the midst of this darkness to over 400,000 witches."

They had a powerful time sharing Jesus in various ways such as praying for the sick, prophesying into their lives and loving on them with honor. The team saw 400 witches be converted and come to our Lord.

John Paul had a long discussion with one of their leaders and she told him this story.

"Many of the witches grew up in Christian homes and attended church regularly. But they were all disillusioned as they never saw or felt two very important things. One was the lack of Christians who really loved, as opposed to just talking about love. The second thing they never saw or experienced was the power of the God in the Bible."

Well, 400 of them saw and experienced the **power** of the God as revealed in the Bible and were **loved** into His kingdom! Now that is the light shining in darkness!

Interestingly enough some churches were there protesting the witches. But John Paul's group went in and demonstrated the very things that the witches were looking for in their spiritual journey—sincere love and true spiritual power. It is a "Love War!"

Beloved we owe it to the world to reveal His love and also His power. Neither of these can happen if you are untrained and untested.

Radical Christianity

Have you ever heard of Leonard Dober or David Nitschmann? I believe that in the eternal history books they will be standing with the Apostle Paul.

In the Moravian community of Herrenhut, founded by Count Nikolaus Ludwig von Zinzendorf in 1732, an amazing thing happened. Because of persecution many Christians from various backgrounds gathered at his estate to worship. [3] Many were Lutheran, Anabaptist, Moravians and Catholics and they gathered together because the Count was willing to give them a place of refuge where they could live peacefully and serve the God of heaven. This little group quickly grew to several hundred people, but those first five years were very shaky. Several times it seemed the whole community would be totally destroyed as the strong opinions of this diverse group continually clashed with one another. Many of them had martyrs in their family heritage. They were people of strong convictions. They had strong **"stand alone muscles."** But the **"blend together muscles"** were not very strong among them.

At this point they had not learned to "complete one another as they were still competing" over doctrinal issues. They all had their theological guns loaded for bear and were using them on each other causing many offenses in the community.

Then in May 1727 after much prayer, fasting, admonition and teaching from the Word of God, Count Zinzendorf convinced them to lay down their theological guns, to look to Christ, the head of the body, and to love one another just the way they were. They became convinced that would never be able to stay together if they kept fussing about all of these things.

From that point the Holy Spirit began to brood over their meetings in a new way. Unified prayers began to rise out of this theological-divided people. In August 1727, a visitation of God came, and they were never the same after that. The whole church was baptized in the fullness of Christ. The whole community was lifted into heavenly realms, and they began to walk there continuously.

That day, in the midst of that unified communion service; they saw the slain Lamb by revelation of the Spirit of God. They saw Jesus. They saw the beautiful Gospel as they had never seen it before. They saw the wounds in his side. They saw the blood that flowed out of His side. They saw the power of that blood. They saw the victory that was in that blood.

Within five years the burden for lost souls was so strong in the community that they sent out their first two missionaries.

Who were the first two missionaries? Leonard Dober, a potter, and David Nitschmann, a carpenter, had such a burden for the slaves in the island of Saint Thomas that they arranged to have themselves **"sold into slavery"** in order that they could reach out and love those slaves with the love of Jesus! Many of the other young men in the community were gravely disappointed because they wanted to be going instead of Leonard and David. Can you imagine selling yourself as a slave into horrible barbaric conditions to showcase the love of our Savior? The constraining love for their own Savior led them to lay down their own life; in order that others might live, and live eternally.

That church is a "Sheepdog" looking over the sheep!

At the dock as they were leaving on their ocean journey they yelled inspiring words back to their family and friends that knew they would never see them again. They all knew that this was a ministry unto death, but for His glory.

They cried out these words: **"May the Lamb that was slain receive the reward of His suffering!"**

Beloved, that is a Love War cry!

A Word of Encouragement for Warriors

Many warriors get snagged by the **transition tension time** between the revelation and the manifestation of reality in their lives. The **transition tension time** is the time between the receiving of the word of revelation and the manifestation of that word. For instance, Joseph had dreams at the age of 12 that revealed he was going to be a ruler, but it was 18 years of character building before Joseph was finally placed in that position. Those 18 years were the **transition tension time**, and a time of walking as a warrior in faith.

Moses spent 40 years on the backside of the desert because he misunderstood the calling and fulfillment of that calling. He decided to trust the arm of his own flesh and in his zeal killed an Egyptian. That act cost him another 40 years of character training in the quietness of the desert and was his **transition tension time.** When he came out of the desert he was a humble man and was not so fast to react in his own wisdom or flesh.

King David did not go immediately from the pasture to the palace. In fact he spent about 13 years being molded into the vessel that God knew He could trust with His kingdom.

Those 13 years were his **transition tension time**, and a time of walking as a warrior in faith.

These three warrior saints, Moses, Joseph and David reveal the glorious truth that there is a transition tension time between the revelation of their calling and the manifestation of their calling. This is normal Christian life. It takes time for us to be prepared to flow in the calling and fulfill the destiny that our King has ordained for us. The wait is always worth it, although it is sometimes a painful process. Remember Joseph? He learned to be faithful through the ministry of the *"toilet bowl brush."* Was it painful to be forcibly separated from your family and friends, forced to do demeaning and degrading work? I am sure that it was.

I remember well that there were a few Marine recruits at Parris Island that thought they were somehow "above" menial labor such as scrubbing the bathroom floor with a toothbrush. It took some longer than others to realize that the DI's were trying to teach them to be faithful in the little things so that they could be given the responsibility of bigger things.

You are never promoted till you pass the test!

We all know that it is true even in school. You don't enter the 5th grade until you pass the 4th grade. And if you fail the 4th grade then you take it over till you pass it. Pretty simple principle. It also true in the spiritual realm as well. Sadly, many dear Christian people spend their entire lives in the 4th grade—not understanding that the tests have to be passed before they are promoted.

How did Joseph get promoted? By being **Faithful** to His God wherever He was. He learned to **Honor** not only those in authority, but all his fellow slaves as well. He did that by first Honoring his God. He **Stood in the Gap** for his slaves, and having passed that test was able to **Stand in the Gap** and become the restorer of his own family as well as the nations!

Fight the good fight of Faith

Fighting the good fight of faith [#4] is the **transition tension time**. This fight of faith or standing in the **transition tension time** was what made the difference in Joseph's life.

My good friend and ministry partner [#5] John Shergur describes the transition tension time like this.

John said it is like a coin. On one side of the coin we have:

- Revelation
- Word
- Truth
- Faith

And on the other side of the coin we have:

- Speculation
- Facts
- Reasoning
- Fears

John and I were on our way to speak at a conference and I was struggling with some issues in my life and was sharing them with him. John sat back and pondered for a moment, and then gave me the word of the Lord. "Ish quit flipping the coin!" He went on and said "You are looking at the wrong side of the coin. You keep seeing with the natural eye the facts, speculation, reasoning and fears when the Lord has shown you the revelation, word and truth concerning the issues. Now walk in Faith!"

That is the **transition tension time**—the time between

the revelation and manifestation of what we know to be true. This is a dangerous time for Warriors as the time of transition is when you are most vulnerable[#6] to the world, the flesh, and the devil. The answer is to *"fight the good fight of faith."*

The same is true with all the other warriors who have fought the *Good Fight of Faith* and it will also be true of us in this hour if we are to win the Love War.

The world is waiting to see His redemption and to experience His love, power and grace. Are you standing in the Gap? Are you standing on the Wall? Have you been trained and tested? Have you walked ***"The Warrior's Walk"*** in the dark places to reveal His love?

Is He tugging at your heart to continue in the battle?

*"On your walls, O Jerusalem, I have
appointed watchmen;*

All day and night they will never keep silent

You, who remind the Lord, take no rest for yourselves!"

(Isaiah 62:6)

Warrior! Do you hear the call? The trumpet is blowing. Our brothers and sons, our daughters and sisters, our families and all of creation are waiting.

To the wall Warriors, Rise up, enter the Fight. The Captain of our Salvation is with us!

Amen

Endnotes: Chapter Twelve

#1- John 1: 4-12

#2- John Paul Jackson % Streams Ministries, Colleyville, TX. www.Streamsministries.com

#3- Much of this research and information came from an article "The Radical Example of Moravian Missions" by Denny Kenaston. Many of these statements are direct quotes from Denny's article. Thank You Denny.

#4- 1 Timothy 6:12a

#5- It is such a blessing to have a brother flowing with you when you minister and travel. In fact it is imperative to have someone you can be accountable to as you walk the walk of faith. God meant for us to do it together and two can put much evil to flight.

#6- 1 John 2:16-17

Please check out our other resources, books, and materials at:
www.Restoringhearts.net.

Ish and Tonda Payne,
Deanne Day,
John and Pam Shergur,
all members of Restoring Hearts Ministry
are available to teach and speak these life changing principles via:
seminars and conferences.
Please contact us to schedule one in your area!

Our hearts desire is to:

"See the wounded soldier in the body of Christ find healing and deliverance, while finding vision and ministry in this end time harvest. We are committed to helping individuals "complete" the vision and ministry that He has called you to."

4702661R0

Made in the USA
Charleston, SC
04 March 2010